THE POWER OF REIKI, CRYSTALS AND SYNCHRONICITY

By Joy Fraser

PREFACE

Have you ever thought a lot of coincidental things happened around you? This happened to me but as time passed after learning reiki, I realised they were not coincidences. Instead they were synchronistic events which kept on happening. I was on holiday a few years ago and met up with the author of the Skellee books. If you have young children, you should check these out. My grandchildren loved them when they were younger. When I was telling her about all the things that happened to me, she said, "You should write a book." I thought this was beyond me and jokingly told her it should be called the never-ending story as these synchronicities would never end. Well, now that time has come, and I hope you will like my muses.

The Reiki Principles

Just for today, do not worry

Just for today, do not anger

Just for today, be kind to all people

Just for today, earn your living honestly

Just for today, show Gratitude to every living thing

Reiki is Universal Life Force

Contents

MY INTRODUCTION TO REIKI

"What is Reiki?" I hear you say. Reiki is an original method of healing using Energy. It was rediscovered and developed by Mikao Usui who lived in Japan early in the 20th Century. Therefore, the original reiki is called Usui Reiki. The word Reiki is made of two Japanese words - Rei which means "God's Wisdom or the Higher Power" and Ki which is "life force energy". So, Reiki is actually "spiritually guided life force energy.

I was first introduced to Reiki by a friend who was taking a Massage Therapy degree course at University. Many people were advising her that she should add Reiki into her therapies, but she told them she did not want to jump on a bandwagon. That was until someone gave her Reiki and she had such a strong reaction that she went ahead and trained. She then asked me to be her Guinea Pig to practice on. During the next few weeks as I lay on her therapy table, she asked what I was feeling. I advised nothing at all. This confused her as she felt so much when she was treating me so in the end, she told me to use it as time out and just relax for an hour. As I was a single mum this was great that I was being given permission to have some time out! This went on for months and she was right that it gave me an hour of complete relaxation, so I did enjoy visiting her. I was lucky because as she went on to train in different therapies, I got to be the guinea pig many times over.

The funny thing about Reiki is the practitioner and the client can both feel different things and sometimes nothing at all, but the energy still works on the recipient. I have since that day found all different types of reactions with both therapists and clients. I have found the best way is to tell clients not to expect anything but just to relax and enjoy the experience. Some of their experiences are surprising even to me. Occasionally a person may not feel any different after the hour but the next day will contact me to say they had the best sleep in a long time. Even if people are not aware, the energy keeps working through and detoxing them for a few days after a session. So, for my introduction to reiki I was one of those that just felt calm and relaxed. I also always slept well after a session.

WHAT REIKI CAN DO FOR YOU

Until now we did not know the full story about Dr Usui due to not enough information coming from Japan, but this is changing. We now know that manuscripts from him and a couple of master's that he trained have been found and soon they will be shared with the western world. Also symbols that are used in Usui reiki are very similar to symbols found in a temple on Mount Karuna. These symbols came into his mind when he was on a 21-day retreat on Mount Karuna. Throughout his education, Dr. Usui had an interest in medicine, psychology and theology. As he was a learned man who had been a public servant, Industrialist, Politicians secretary, missionary and a Tendai monk amongst other things and travelled to western countries and China, it is likely that he picked up a lot of information on his travels and brought them all together and this all came together on the mountain and became Usui reiki – named after him. It is also believed that other styles of reiki were being practised in Japan around the same time.

Dr Usui opened a clinic in Japan to treat people either for free or at a low cost. His work became more publicised after an earthquake in 1923 where over 140,000 people were killed. He then worked very hard with his helpers to help as many people as they possibly could. One of his helpers was a man called Chujiro Hayashi. It is believed that he was the person who came up with the hand positions for giving a treatment. We know that it does not matter where your hands are laid, either on or above the body, as the energy will go to where it is needed. When being taught this way, it helps the students to be aware of where the Chakras are (energy points) so that they can learn to get more information from the body. The chakras are like spinning wheels and when the body is out of sorts, they can become sluggish and make you feel unwell. Reiki can help realign the chakras, helping people to become more balanced. I have many times had it shown to me that clients still feel as if my hands are on one place on the body when I have already moved on. They are even more amazed if they feel me at one end, and when they open their eyes, see me at the opposite side of them. The energy works with what the body needs.

Reiki can help to bring balance to the mind and emotions and helps give a feeling of wellbeing on all levels. Reiki is safe and natural and is now used in many hospitals all over the world. It can be used for pregnant women, the elderly, babies and animals. The energy can also be used on food, drinks and plants. In fact, it has unlimited uses and can be used in all situations. It can also give people a zest for living and help them make the changes to have a more positive outlook in life. I have had students getting watches and clocks to start working again after learning reiki. I always remember my teacher advising he was in a car with a student and the car broke down. After pulling up the bonnet and trying different things he got back in the car defeated. His student then suggested they used reiki on the car. The student teaching the teacher! We are all learning constantly. Guess what? After using reiki, he put the key in the ignition, and it started first time.

A reiki therapist cannot claim to heal any illness, but the energy will work with the body and mind to give what it needs at that point in time. One of my pet hates is if people call me a Healer. The energy is the healer and the person is only a conduit to allow the energy to access the body. It can also give those that are about to pass over a peaceful transition through acceptance. Reiki is now used in many hospitals and hospices across the world. It is good to see it becoming more mainstream. There have been scientific experiments done which show when someone is giving reiki, the client's energy levels increase to the same higher vibration as the therapist. More and more times in recent years I see published articles that show how reiki is being used in controlled settings and having great outcomes.

SEEING REIKI IN ACTION

Reiki can be given either seated or lying down. It can even be sent over distance. There is no reason to disrobe. I would suggest removing shoes and glasses and making yourself comfortable. Some people like to listen to music during a therapy session, others prefer silence. There is no one way that fits all. Sometimes people want to talk about what they are feeling either physically or emotionally. At other times people will be so relaxed that they will fall asleep. The important thing here is to go with what you, as a client, wish. I often find the birds outside my house joining in and so many people have said they like the bird music. The other interesting thing is if I hear a noise such as a fire engine going past, and at the end of the session I apologise for the noise, many times clients have been so chilled out they have not heard any external noises at all.

A year or so after being my friend's guinea pig I was co-ordinating a reiki workshop for a social group called SPICE. You should check this group out as it is UK wide. It stands for Special Programme of Initiative, Challenge and Excitement. During this evening, the Reiki Master had everyone sitting on chairs with our hands touching the shoulders of the people in front of us. There were about 6 rows of us. He then touched the first person gently. Within minutes people were saying they had heat, coldness, tingling or other sensations in areas where they had health problems. All I heard was "I had heat in my shoulder, I had a cold feeling in my knee, I had tingling in my foot". We were amazed that the energy was so strong that it was going through everyone by him touching only one person!

Later, that evening, after I had tidied away the chairs and everyone had left, I stopped to speak to him. I had a bad back problem and after sitting in the hard chair for three hours I was in agony. It was winter, and I had on warm clothes and my Jacket as I was ready to leave. He asked if I had a few minutes to sit down which I did. He then put his hands on my back, and I felt heat going through my Jacket. Through the heat, I felt my back-pain lessening until it disappeared completely. I was completely blown away. After suffering from back problems for over ten years, here was something that could help me. I was hooked!

MY TRUE TEACHER

I decided after that evening to be trained in Reiki. I went for a couple of sessions with this teacher and then booked in a date to be trained to Level One Usui Reiki. An interesting thing happened on one of my visits for a therapy session though. I had taken a friend with me and she was sitting in the corner of the room. On this occasion I was feeling nothing and then I heard a sound coming from her corner. The energy had decided to work on her rather than me! She had Crystals in her pocket and felt the energy coming to her. It was so strong it was making her gasp. The reiki master advised that she must have needed it more than me. As you can guess I was a little upset as I had paid for the session. We soon had a laugh about it. I now know it is better to go in alone.

I could hardly contain my excitement as it got closer to the date of my workshop. I then received a phone call to advise me that not enough people had signed up for the workshop in my home town of Edinburgh and would I like to go to one an hour away in Glasgow on a different date? I was devastated as I wanted neither of these. I had in my mind the date I was to be attuned and it had to be local to me. I had no idea at the time why I was feeling this way, but more was to become clearer as I went down this path.

Thinking of my friend I went and asked her who her teacher was and then called him. Unbelievably he was having a workshop on the date I had already pencilled in my diary to learn level one. Synchronicity at its best! He also only had another two people that he was training that day. I immediately thought this was a sign, as he did not cancel for small numbers and agreed to be trained by him. It was the best decision of my life and I owe the way my life has progressed to him. The day was fantastic. I remember giving a total stranger (one of the other students) reiki and felt the energy going to a part of his body. He advised this was an area where he had an ongoing problem. He was astonished, as was I, when he pinpointed an old injury I had as well. I was so excited after this day that I couldn't wait to try it out on others. I remember going home and it felt like I could not get the reiki to switch on. I felt sad thinking maybe I was only going to be able to do it at David's' house. Maybe there was something magical about it that I did not have in my home. I have since heard this from others so believe it must just be coming down from all the energy of the day. I did sleep well that night.

With any reiki training you have a twenty-one-day cleansing period to practise on yourself. A lot of changes can take place during this time which can include problems that you have buried in the past coming back to be resolved. I sometimes find that people can feel down for a few days then they experience an enormous high. They then tell me that they feel so positive and calm, so the few days were worth it. Others just sail through the process feeling fantastic from day one. I recently found my write up of my cleansing period. It was interesting looking back on how I was after my level one training. I had a few off days, then felt as if the world was a much brighter place to live in.

TIME FOR CHANGE

I remember going to walk in my local park the day after my attunement. The colours were more vibrant and all I could hear were the sounds of nature. I had never taken notice of these things before. I became more aware of everything around me and the beauty of nature. I recognised the sounds of the different birds, including to my surprise, a Woodpecker. This has continued up till now, all these years later. Until then a park had just been a place to walk my dog. I would also walk quickly to get from A to B, so this was something new for me. While I was walking through the park, I felt my hands buzzing as the energy switched on. I looked around me to see who needed reiki but could see no one else.

When I got home, I was walking round the house giving reiki to all my plants. It was if a light had been turned on. I felt I had to give energy to everything. I especially decided to test it by using on one of my tall plants that was due to be binned thinking it was too far gone to be saved. Imagine my delight when after three days it started to look better. After three weeks you would not have known it had ever been a sick plant. In fact, it became so healthy that in the end it towered above its companion plant. How I loved my reiki. The use of reiki is limitless. It can be used for so much.

When I mentioned the time out walking in the park to my teacher, he advised that as there was only me who had been in the park, then the reiki must have been meant for me. I have since found if this happens, all I do is put my hands in my pockets and then I can feel this wonderful energy flowing through me. It's something that I always pass on to my students too now.

I was to get a big surprise though as I found I was able to help others, but not my own back problem, after being trained in level one. I found this frustrating. The interesting thing was my friend, who I had never felt anything from when receiving Reiki, was now able to give such strong Reiki that she was able to help my back whenever I needed it. I remember one time when I had a funeral to go to and my back went big time and I could not stand up. After sitting with her hands on my back for 30 minutes I was able to get through not only the funeral but the wake afterwards. I was very confused about now feeling it from my friend but not being able to do this for myself. I had gone through Usui level one expecting to have the power to help myself and it had not happened. This was to be explained to me later.

Part of the level one training is being told of the Reiki principles that we should try to live by, and I have incorporated these into my life. It is amazing that just changing your mind set can make such a difference in your life. I think that even if those not prac-tising reiki abided by these ideals that the world would be a much happier place.

THE FIVE PRINCIPLES OF REIKI

Just for today, do not worry.

Worry changes nothing. If it has already happened, you cannot change it. If it is in the future it may not happen.

Just for today, do not anger.

Anger only hurts you. Take a step back or walk away from the situation / conversation.

Just for today, be kind to all people.

Having respect for others allows you to have greater respect for yourself. I always tell students that even if someone has upset them, they should send love in that direction.

Earn your living honestly.

Living your life this way means you are living as you should. I know if I did something wrong it would come back to bite me!

Show gratitude to every living thing.

Once you try, you can always find reasons to be Grateful. Everything living thing has a purpose on Earth, so we should be grateful for them being here with us.

I am seen by many people now as a calm person who is not quick to anger. This was a big learning curve for me especially as my life was not so good up to that point. I will give you a laugh though. I am so conscious of the honesty part that one Christmas at work we were doing a Secret Santa and had written up three things we might like bought for us. One thing I love is Yankee candles, so this was on my list. I then heard someone in the office was selling these cheaper than normal and asked why. Apparently, they had fallen off the back of a lorry. I then worried that someone would get me one and I would not be able to use it just in case it was one of those. Luckily, I got a totally different make of candle, so I could relax and enjoy it when Santa came.

One of the interesting things I have found with reiki is you do not know where it will take you when you start out. Many people stop after level one as this is all they need. It improves people's lives in so many ways that they are happy with the first level and do not feel the need to take it forward. I love that after one day's training it can make such a difference for people. Learning reiki has taught me more than anything, to live in the present. Of course, that does not stop us making long term goals, but it does make you appreciate where you are now.

I can only say that over time thoughts kept coming into my mind again and again about level two. I had not expected that I would want to go on to the next level, but it seems that I was being directed to do this as there came a time I could not stop thinking of level two. I decided to save up for this and see what I was meant to be taught. I strongly believe that if anything keeps coming back into your mind it is for a reason. Throughout my years with reiki this has happened time and again so now I always act on the thoughts.

LEVEL TWO

A few months later I went to the same teacher, David Tyrrell, to be trained to level two. Again, this was only a very small class and I mentioned to him that I felt confused that reiki level one had not helped me but enabled me to help others. People were saying the energy felt very strong when receiving from me, but it was not helping my back at all. He then asked me if anyone had mentioned that the way I behaved or talked had changed? He told me that he had noticed a big change in me. After thinking about this I said that yes there was a difference. Before level one everything was going wrong in my life and I was anxious for much of the time. I realised how much happier I was with my life now. I was astonished when he told me the energy would go to where it was needed most, not where I had expected or wanted it to go to. It had been working all this time on my mind and I found that I was now a much more positive person than I had been before. I had learned my first lesson. This has been proved time and time again to me since that period when I have treated both myself and clients. Often the energy goes where the client did not expect but when we meet up again, I am advised it was the right thing for them at that time. It may be that someone has stomach aches. Sometimes the energy will concentrate on the head. In those cases, the stomach problem was caused by stress from what was going on in the persons mind.

I was also of the mind-set that if two things had gone wrong, I was just waiting for the third bad thing to happen. How many of us think this way? I hear this, especially in the workplace. If the day started off bad, I would hear people say the rest of the day would continue in the same way. This had now changed for me. I realised it was all about mindset and that after a bad start to the day, it could only get better! This is a much better way of looking at any situation. I always said that if you had a bad call it was a one off. There is no reason to believe that every call after that would be the same. Why do people think that way?

So, in the end reiki level one had turned out to be a positive experience for me. It may seem strange, but it has completely changed the way I see life. Nothing is insurmountable in my life now. I know that I am in the right place at the right time and there is no reason to get stressed. Level one had concentrated on my mind rather than my back and for that I am very grateful.

One thing that had been wrong in my life during that time had been my roof which had been leaking for a while. I had paid three companies to try to fix it with no success. This had me very worried as water was coming into the house and damaging the walls inside. I had not realised, but after training in level one my whole mind-set had changed. Now instead of being anxious I had the attitude of "It's okay, everything will turn out fine" and I did not worry. The roof did eventually get fixed and out of that I got a new Therapy space in my attic to chill out which a friend built for me.

Another thing happened around this time. I had written a blog and I advised that I no longer watched the news on TV but did view it as writing on my laptop. This way you can read without the emotional embellishment that the reporters add to their scripts. After I mentioned this way of thinking to a friend, he thought the same and said if you were meant to hear any news it would come to you at the right time. The very next day I logged into my BT Yahoo site and it had all changed. The sites that I had on there to give me news had disappeared! Instead of the BBC news and my local Newspaper pages it was now blank. After a few minutes of trying to get them back on again I sat back for a moment and had a light bulb moment. A higher source had decided I did not need to see any news at all at this moment in time.

Since then the only time I catch any news is if I switch on the radio and it comes on. I immediately change channel, so I do not have my positive mental attitude decreased. I find even listening to a few seconds saddens me as it's usually bad news. I did have a couple of days of wanting my fix, but this has now gone, and I am amazed how much lighter I feel now. I have now not watched television or listened to the news for 7 years!

The most amazing thing that I have found recently is many more people are thinking the same way in wanting to stay positive and not be pulled down by negative news. I spoke to someone recently who said he has not seen or heard the news in years too. It's as if a shift is taking place. In actual fact I have been finding a lot more sites that I am being drawn to that are full of good news stories instead. In these days of social media, you get lots of news stories popping up. As I don't trust a lot of what I see, if I'm interested, I do my own research. One of the things you should always do is check the source before sharing news items. Even then you may find the source to be corrupted. Many of the news stories are there to instil fear into us all. It's also important to be aware that what you are seeing may be manipulated. We have all seen the same people that pop up at different war zones!

It's important to be aware that more often good things happen than bad. It seems though, that bad stories make people read newspapers and watch the news on T.V. Since I made the decision to stop watching television it was the best thing for me at that time and it still is.

ABLE TO CONTROL PAIN

When I trained in level two, I was finally able to come off my daily painkillers. I remember my back hurting when I was sitting at my desk. All I needed to do now was place my hands on my legs under my desk at work and no one knew I was giving myself reiki. It is important to know that reiki can be used at any given time or moment. You need no special equipment to carry with you either-just yourself. I often tell people they can give themselves reiki on the bus or train in the morning if they are rushed, but somehow, they should always make time out of their day to give themselves reiki. I now had the means to control my pain by giving myself reiki whenever I needed it. I felt released from my monthly visits to the Osteopath and if my back let me down, I recovered so much faster. This coupled with the fact I now had a much more positive attitude meant the start of a new life for me.

With level two under my belt I was able to do so many different things. I was happy to help spread the word of how much reiki can help people to relax and chill out. I also found as the reiki grew stronger, so synchronicity kept happening to me.

One big part of training in level two is the ability to send the reiki over distance and time. On the day I was trained I had picked a photo from all the photos and pieces of paper that the teacher had face down on a table for people to send reiki to. To my surprise the photo I had chosen was of a Boxer dog. After sending reiki

I advised I had felt it going to the head and the stomach area. I was then told it was a dog who loved reiki and she had just given birth. There was a problem with her womb and the puppies were doing her head in! In fact, she was just around the corner from where I was sitting. What a day of experiences that was – a totally magical day. The interesting thing about that dog was she would walk backwards towards her master and wait for him to give her reiki. When she decided she had enough she would walk away. I was pleased that I had chosen such a lovely dog to work with. It was also my first experience of sending it over distance to a person as we did this for a couple of people as well. Imagine being able to say what I felt and having it corroborated by the person I sent the energy to. I had loved my level one workshop but level two exceeded my expectations. After this workshop, I worked even more on myself. I practiced sending reiki into my past. Many things had happened in preceding years that still bothered me were then able to be dealt with. These were things that I thought I had moved past, but all I had done up till then was bury them at the back of my mind. With the help of reiki, I was finally able to release myself from the emotions that were attached.

DISTANCE REIKI

My next momentous time of using distance reiki was when my whole team at work had to reapply for our jobs and go through an interview process along with others who wanted to join the team. This was now being opened to the whole company, which meant thousands of people. It was a big shock as previously we had been told that if we made it past three months, we would become permanent in that role. Everyone was anxious as we had believed the jobs were guaranteed after a year of working in the team. On talking to my reiki teacher about this he reminded me I could send reiki to the situation. He also advised both he and my friend Anne would send it also. Before I left home in the morning, I sent reiki to my workplace. This is the great thing about reiki. You can send it to places as well as people, at a time in the future, as well as to the past.

As I walked through the door at work a complete blanket of calm surrounded me. I had never felt so relaxed and happy. I cannot really put it into words, but it was as if my whole body was covered in light and a feeling of peace. It brought to my attention just how powerful this energy was. Throughout the morning my colleagues were going for their interview and returning to let us know how they had got on. There was always something they thought should have been communicated better to the interviewers or that they had missed saying something important. Not one person was completely happy about their interview. When it was my time, I was cool, calm and collected. On returning from my interview I was asked what I could have done better. I said nothing at all. Everything had gone the way I wanted. They did not believe this and kept saying that there must be at least one question that I had not liked. I can honestly say I had a feeling that everything will be all right and was not stressed in the slightest.

One of my colleagues had Dyslexia and had got himself into a real state and asked if whatever I had taken could be given to him too. When I went home for lunch, I sent him distance reiki and he sailed through his interview. The good news was most of us were able to keep our jobs. Many people use level two for just themselves, but I love being able to help friends, family and colleagues. Better still I do not need any equipment to help me either.

This same colleague used to jokingly call me a witch until a certain day. His wife had an awful pregnancy and the baby was possibly needing to be born at a specialist hospital. In the end they allowed him to be born at the local one, but he needed a lot of help. One day this friend came to me with two photographs. One of his (I think three-year-old) and one of the new born. As soon as I held the photos, my hand holding the baby photo started buzzing. He asked me what was wrong, and I said the baby wanted energy but of course I would not do that as I knew his father did not still totally believe in reiki. He asked me to please send energy to his baby in the hospital. I sat down and did this but then the boss came back, so I said I would send more later.

The next day he came and said, "I know when you sent reiki last night!" He said he had picked the baby up who was a little blue and he felt a ball of light going up through the baby and turning his skin pink again. I had to tell him that when I went to send it, the baby told me he did not need any more. After that day he certainly believed in reiki and sometimes even now he gets me to send reiki to himself. His world has come full circle. He took up Yoga and said the teacher was drawing funny symbols at the end of his sessions. I said to ask if they were reiki symbols and the answer was "yes". It is good that he feels so comfortable amongst energy these days. I can even see him training in reiki himself in the future.

People who have never learned reiki struggle with believing distance reiki! This can come in very handy for unresolved issues in the previous years of someone's life. I have had people tell me that they felt the strings that kept them attached to a person or problem now felt cut, as if a weight had been removed from their shoulders. One thing that should be remembered is if you feel attachment to a problem or the way someone spoke to or treated you, then the only person that is being hurt is yourself. Many people, after sending reiki, say they can now look back at a problem but no longer feel upset or angry about it. That is a good result.

I remember wanting to see if Emotional Freedom Technique (EFT) was something I would be interested in being trained in. The person running the workshop suggested I paid her a couple of visits to see what it was all about. Half way through she asked again if I had done this before and I advised that I had never touched EFT before that day. She asked why I had no unresolved issues to my past if I had not used EFT. I told her that any issues had been resolved with me sending reiki to the past and believe me there had been quite a few issues to resolve. She found this hard to believe and kept insisting I must have used EFT in the past. She was wrong! After doing an introduction course to EFT with her I decided that it was not for me. I know many people that use EFT and get a lot out of it so don't let that put you off.

REIKI FROM THE BEGINNING OF LIFE

Reiki is used every day in my life. I wake up in the morning and give myself reiki and fall asleep doing the same. One part that gives me lots of enjoyment is being able to help my family. When my daughter was pregnant with her first child there were complications in that the baby kept being still for too long and she had to visit her local doctor and hospital quite a lot. That was until we found out if I laid my hands on her the baby started to do somersaults. This saved us many anxious moments. Nearer to the birth he went quiet again and this time my daughter wanted to go to the hospital to get checked. They wired her up to all the equipment. The doctor examined her and had a very concerned look on her face. The equipment did not appear to be picking anything up either. As the doctor left the room to get a second opinion, we were both holding our breath and then my daughter started to panic and asked me to give her reiki. The great thing was to see the machines all kick into action and you could see and hear all the baby's movements on them. When the doctors came back into the room, they advised us to go for a walk to calm the baby down as it was now too active! What a relief that was.

One night a few months after the birth of my first healthy grandchild I was in bed when I was called at midnight to say the baby would not stop crying and was running a very high temperature as well as being distressed so they were on the way to the hospital. The next day my daughter called and asked me if I had sent reiki after she had spoken to me and I confirmed I had. She told me the baby stopped crying within moments. We have since found that both her children get really high temperatures when they are sick. I always remember a time that his temperature was sky high and I was taking them to our local hospital. As we went outside in the cool air his temperature came down quite a bit. When we arrived at the hospital the doctor took his temperature and said it was very high. We advised it had been higher than that which he found difficult to accept. Since then he has been admitted to hospital, so the doctors have seen for themselves how high it really goes up to.

EXCITING TIMES

Many people train in level one and decide that is all they need. Those who go on to level two sometimes want to be able to treat members of the public and be paid for this. When I did level two, I just felt the need to use the energy for myself and my family. I never thought I would want to take it any further and for the next two years I was content with this. Then the synchronicity continued. I had been visiting a crystal shop for a couple of years and the couple running it decided to take over the shop next door and make it into a therapy room. It had been a dream of theirs for years. As many therapists over the years had visited and left business cards with them, they had got to know them all well. They made the decision to ask five or six therapists that they gelled with to work in the therapy shop and I was chosen to be one of them at weekends, so I could continue my day job. The therapy shop was filled with billowing sales from the ceiling and lovely ambient lighting, including a lovely colour changing light which I now have in my therapy room. Until this point, I had never thought of using reiki outside the circle of family and friends. This was my next learning curve.

My new therapy space came about as I used my home for foreign language students to stay with me all year round. One day I was complaining to one of the shop owners that I had no "me" space anymore as all my rooms were taken. He mentioned my attic and I gave him the sad story. He advised me once my attic was fixed to let him know and he would build a corner of it into a space for me to meditate. When I advised him months later that it was now sorted, he spent a few days in my attic and said I was not allowed to look. He then took me shopping for some wood panelling. When it was finished, I absolutely loved it. He not only gave me a meditation space, he also converted the whole attic into a wonderful space for me. The atmosphere in it is wonderful, plus his wife made me an Angel from feathers to hang from my window and my Son in law made me a Fairy Door for it too. I was later, after becoming more comfortable, able to use it for clients as well.

Soon after this I had a spiritual reading from my teacher David and was advised that he saw I had a spare room in my house and was seen to be treating people sitting on a chair. He did not know if this was friends or clients. At the time I was not comfortable treating strangers in my home. After a while I decided to think about it and determined to get myself a therapy bed for the room even though David had not seen a bed. On checking out prices I thought I would not be able to afford one. That Christmas an aunt gave me unexpected money for Christmas by doubling what she had previously given me, and I then saw brand new Therapy beds on eBay for auction and managed to get one for the money I now had. Initially this was used to have exchange visits with my friend and other therapists. It was not until later that it was opened to the public. I have since found that often, all I need do is put a thought out there and it materialises in time.

Since then I have never looked back and love treating clients in my home. Often, I will chat for quite a bit after the therapy session. I feel gratitude that I do not make all my living from reiki. This means I do not have back to back clients and can enjoy their company after the therapy session if required. It never ceases to amaze me how much reiki helps people and often people want to talk more in depth about it. Sometimes they decide to learn to do it themselves and the next time I see them it can be for a reiki workshop.

CRYSTALS

Now with my work in the therapy shop I was introduced to all sorts of crystals and found out some fascinating things. While I had been in a bad marriage, I had been drawn to collecting jewellery all made of Hematite. At that time, I just thought it was pretty. I never even knew it was a crystal. I found out that this is a grounding and protecting crystal. The interesting thing is when my marriage came to an end the pieces of jewellery starting breaking or one half of a pair of earrings would mysteriously disappear. I now no longer needed the protection of the hematite and was happy to explore other crystals to wear and built up a lovely collection of all colours which I could use depending on my mood or need. Another interesting thing that happens with the crystal Amber is I cannot keep it. Any jewellery that I get given decides to remove itself from me. I always remember a friend giving me a beautiful Amber pendant. The first time I wore it to work, by the time I had got there it had fallen off on the way. This was the last time I ever used Amber. Interestingly I found out that the crystal has these properties. I had got rid of the negative energy, had no headaches, was calm and patient. You get my meaning, I didn't need this crystal in my life.

- *Balances emotions.*
- *Attracts good luck.*
- *Eliminates fears.*
- *Relieves a headache.*
- *Clears the mind.*
- *Dissolves negative energy.*
- *Helps develop patience and wisdom.*

One incident that took place in the therapy shop was me going in to treat a client. As I stood over the therapy table, I felt sick and believed I was being pulled over. On looking underneath, one of the other therapists had left a large ball of Obsidian which is a grounding stone. After that, we made sure that all crystals were removed once someone had finished with a client! Crystals can have super strong energy.

I decided to explore more about crystals and the first book I bought was The Crystal Bible by Judy hall. This explains crystals in an informative way. You can look under properties or colours. It's often my first "go to" book when I am trying to find the right crystal to use for anything. I then went on to read more of her books which include more "New Age" crystals. Crystals are really nothing new as the Egyptians used them too.

This then led me to want to learn more about using crystals for our health and I heard about a crystal course so decided to sign up for it. Before I went on the course, I decide to visit a crystal therapist. At that stage I had no idea what was to take place. I certainly got a surprise but think that synchronicity once again played out. I was a member of a metaphysical group. This was a group where we talked about many interesting subjects including ghosts and out of body experiences as well as reiki and meditation. The person running it had relocated to Edinburgh, and as she had set one up in her last city decided it was our time. Guess what she was? That's right - she was a crystal therapist!

The crystal therapist I visited had a selection of very big crystals in the room and gave me some interesting information about them. One was a massive Smokey Quartz and as it was used over time, was becoming clearer and clearer. It was the first time I had been aware that could happen. She also had crystals that were record keepers and she advised me they all had a story to tell. She told me a story of taking a client into another room to put his hands on a large quartz crystal. Just as she left him there holding the crystal the doorbell rang. She ended up having a long conversation on the door step- approximately forty minutes, totally forgetting about her client! When she returned to the room to apologise to the client, he replied that he thought only five minutes had passed. The power of crystals can be amazing.

I lay down not knowing what to expect as she gave me a crystal to hold and placed others around me. At this point I was very surprised to find out that she was also clairvoyant. She started giving me information about my past life while treating me during the therapy hour. Funnily enough It all made sense to me. I was also buzzing with the energy of the crystals she used on and around me. I was now looking forward to the crystal course even more.

During the Melody Crystal course one of the things we were taught was past life ascension which takes you back in time for you to find information to help you today. This is not the same as past life regression as the emotions do not become involved. Guess where I went? I was back to the situation the crystal therapist had spoken to me about. I remember saying I did not want to do the same things as I had done in the past which was taking care of a sick mistress. I then realised at this point, many people that come to me for therapy have various health issues, so in a way I am continuing in the same vein. The only difference now is I have a life outside my clients. Even though I love working with reiki clients, a good work / life balance is important.

When I went home after the course finished my head was full of information for me to practise so I started with friends and family. My experience with my daughter was amazing and gave us both a lot to discuss. I am sure most mothers do not get opportunities like this with their children, but this was only the beginning. The interesting part of this was she saw someone reading a book but could not work out what it was. After spending a few minutes, she was able to see it was a book that I had given her to read about reiki. She said that was her reminder to get reading it.

I was blown away but how much I learned in such a short time about all the ways you can use crystals to change your life and even get information from the past, but I also wanted to learn more about the basics of the different types of crystals and what they could be used for. Around this time my daughter became pregnant. My friend Anne had started to use Pendulums and asked if my daughter would give permission to try and learn the sex of the baby. We were all excited to see the outcome. When Anne asked it was a girl the pendulum moved in a way to indicate "no". When asked about a boy it started swinging wildly in the other direction. I asked if I could try and went through the same questions, but I did not get the same answers. It answered "can't decide" to both questions from me. I then changed the question and asked if it was going to give me an answer. At this point it went very strongly in the "no" direction. It seems that as grandmother to be it decided I should wait for the birth to find out if I was going to have a grandson or granddaughter!

Soon after this, my reiki teacher was holding a crystal workshop, and it was here that I was introduced to using a crystal pendulum properly. He had hidden things in his garden such as bottles of essential oils and we had to find them by asking the pendulum to give a sign for yes and no. Sure enough after asking things such as "Is it in this area?" and getting a "no" answer I would move on by asking more questions and was finally taken to see my crystal that I was to find halfway up a tree. I remember to this day David coming up to me as I was standing looking silly. He asked me if I had a problem. I advised the crystal pendulum had said my item was not to the left or right of where I was standing. Apparently, it was exactly where I was now, but I could not see it. He advised me to look up and sure enough my bottle of essential oils was up in a tree directly above my head. What a fun day that was.

As all energy vibrates at different frequencies, reiki and crystals are no different, and I often use them together when I am treating clients. I sometimes use pendulums to check if people's Chakras (energy points) need a little attention. I then use one to check which the correct crystals to use are. It's amazing how I will be told no, no, then yes as I lay my hands on the right crystal for my clients. These can all then help rebalance the body. One of my favourite crystals is Blue lace agate which can help with communication. It's great if you must stand in front of a lot of people or need to have an awkward conversation with someone. I remember a teacher telling me she always carried a piece as she did a lot of talking to adults. When another teacher asked for help with a discussion she needed to lead, the other let her borrow her crystal. The second teacher felt confident enough to go on and do her talk.

Many crystals have specific properties to help with problems. These may be depression, infertility, nightmares, grounding- the list goes on and on. As I mentioned, my first crystal book was The Crystal Bible by Judy Hall. To this day it is one that I use the most. Funny enough when I was looking for names for my two new puppies a few years later I thought of Merlin for the male. The next day I picked up the Crystal Bible and saw that months before I even thought of getting puppies, I had placed a piece of paper in the page for Merlinite. It was obviously the correct name for him.

Through my love of crystals, I introduced one of my grandsons to them. I remember the first time he visited the crystal shop and was given enough money to buy two crystals. He bought two of the same which were Amethyst. The shop owner told him to pick another two for free, so he chose two Blue Lace Agate. I found this interesting as I thought he would have picked four different crystals. When we got back to my home, he kept transferring the agate from one hand to another and we chatted. My daughter advised he had a problem the previous night when he was meant to talk to his father over the phone. He had advised he wanted to talk but couldn't. Funnily enough Blue Lace Agate helps communication problems and that evening he was then able to speak to his father. I was then advised he had been suffering nightmares. Once again, he had chosen the correct crystal in Amethyst. This is the same grandson that wanted to train in reiki. I think he has a real affinity with crystals and energy. He now has a collection of crystals both from me and those he has bought himself. He loves the crystals so much that he has acquired all his mother's crystals as well. His younger sister also now collects crystals although she does not have as big an interest in them. It's interesting that from having reiki in the womb and loving crystals he went on to also train in reiki.

Even though reiki helped me kill the pain in my back it did not stop it going into crisis for the simplest thing. My back was a problem for me as I could not do many things in my life and I was always frightened that my back would go again by doing the simplest thing. A short time before it went again, someone had introduced me to the Sun Ancon Chi Machine.

SUN ANCON CHI MACHINE

I love how we have so many ways to help ourselves and the right person comes into our lives at the right time. The Chi machine was invented by a doctor of oxygen in Japan. He wanted to help people get more oxygen into their bodies without them having to exercise. He saw Koi Carp swimming in a figure of eight and soon after helped a person by swinging her legs in the same way. After this, he went on to invent the first Chi machine. It is now used worldwide and in hospitals too. I remember being told of a patient's group in a hospital buying one for the staff to use during their breaks. Another eye surgeon let his patients use the machine before they were operated on. The chi machine both gives more energy to people and helps them relax. They also found during trials that it removed excess fluid from the body which was very helpful for people suffering from Lymphoedema. What's not to like in this machine?

The person that introduced me to the chi machine probably does not know how much of an impact this made on my life. He advised me that he had suffered from Cancer and that had caused him to have back problems, so it may help me too and he was right. This also came about synchronically. I met him through my social group on a holiday. He was from England and without the group I would never have met him or heard about this machine. I decided to do a lot more research on the Sun Ancon Chi machine. I found it was the original one and many years had gone into research before making it, so I was completely comfortable about spreading the word and decided to become a distributor of it.

This machine can help many health issues as it gives you a gentle massage and a boost of energy at the end. The most important point for me is it was also a form of exercise that would not put my back out. Once I started using it, I wanted to shout from the rooftops the response my body was getting from it. After eight weeks I had forgotten I had a bad back.

When my daughter was married a few months later I had danced the twist with my other two-year-old grandson. Of course, my back did not like this and went into crisis mode again.

The most unfortunate thing was my Osteopath was on holiday and the two osteopaths that I saw told me not to use my chi machine and to apply cold to my back. As before I had always given myself warm baths and used my chi machine, I should not have been surprised that my back did not improve. When my own practitioner returned the damage was done and it took seven weeks for my back to recover. Before this I had only needed one or two days away from my workplace. He advised me I should have done what I normally did and to stick to this in the future. The people I had seen while he was away had treated me for a new injury when it was referred pain from my existing problems. The good thing was my work was very accommodating and allowed me to take my chi machine into work so that every hour or two I could relax the muscles in my back which allowed me to stay in the office. Since that day I have seen him only a couple of times, just to check all is okay if my back goes, and he always tells me just to keep using the chi machine.

One day I had a therapy event to go with my chi machines and thought how could I do this? My back had gone while I was putting a bottle of water into a bag. How could I even drive to the place? I did not think I would be able to sit in a car, never mind drive. I used the Sun Ancon Chi machine in my home and then got someone to take it out to the car. I was then able to drive forty minutes. As soon as I got to the destination, I had this person set up my exercise mat and machine and went straight back on it again. After ten minutes I was able to stand all day till 4.30pm before I started having problems again. This machine is a miracle worker for me.

You can see what was happening here. All the things that helped me with my health were to do with energy. The crystals, reiki and the Sun Ancon Chi machine were giving me tools not only to help myself but others too. I often find now that clients like to use reiki and crystals at the same time and then they finish off with some time on the Sun Ancon Chi Machine.

After I had recovered, I wanted to make more people aware of the chi machine and started taking it into the therapy shop with me at the weekends. It helps people to relax and chill out, so they did not need to have any health issues. One memory I have is when we were having a weekend of taster sessions. One lady advised me she had many mental health problems. After speaking to her and realising that the issues were severe, and she had not been attending her clinic, I advised that I could not give 15 minutes of reiki as I thought she may become emotional and need a lot more time which I did not have on that day. I suggested she use the chi machine instead. After a few minutes she was lying very relaxed and asked me if the machine would work with the drug Speed. I asked her why and was astounded by her answer. She had taken some just before she entered the therapy shop! I asked her how she was feeling, and she advised very chilled out, so I told her she had the answer - not that I would recommend this to anyone. She also asked that I told her husband in the car waiting on her that she was too relaxed to move. I often find after using the machine that people are so relaxed, they just want to stay on the floor, but this took it to a new limit!

I have since found that the Sun Ancon chi machine is great for people who are stressed or have mental health issues. One of my friends had a highly stressful job and could not switch off at night. When she tried the machine, she said her head felt empty for the first time in years. I have frequently been told by clients that it clears their minds and I can attest to this too. I have found also it helps people with MS, ME and Fibromyalgia. It is unfortunate at this time that more and more people are being diagnosed with the latter two. I think we are living in a sick world now with the amount of pollution and chemicals we put into our bodies daily. This is bound to be influencing our bodies. Also, more and more people are being found to have mental health issues and depression. I think many people struggle to live with the high levels of stress they or circumstances put upon them these days too.

I was lucky to be able to take the chi machines into my work with a national company during their Health and Wellbeing days and it was great to see people getting chilled out within minutes. I remember one lady tell me her baby had finally gone to sleep while she was lying on the floor. It had been very restless up till that point. I told her my daughter went through a period in her pregnancy that the baby kept waking her in the middle of the night. She found if she got out of the bed and went on the chi machine for a few minutes the baby went back to sleep. As she also had pelvic dysplasia, she found it helped immensely with this as well.

I especially remember a day at work when we were in a room that if there was no movement, the energy efficient lights would go off. I had three people lying on the floor and switched on all their machines. Within a couple of minutes, the lights switched off. When the machines finally switched off the clients lay still as I had advised. The atmosphere was so peaceful, and everyone was relaxed until one of them moved and the lights all switched back on again. All I heard then was "bright lights, bright lights!" It was quite funny.

Usually when I took the chi machines into the office, I would have all my colleagues standing watching those using the machines as it looks quite funny when you see people's bodies moving in a figure of eight. They would then goad all their friends to take a session on the chi machines. Feedback was always good; in fact, one person said to me that if they had a call with a member of the public that upset them then a few minutes on this machine would clear their heads and calm them down. Perhaps a Sun Ancon chi machine should be in every workplace. If you want to check it out information can be found on my website here: https://peaceharmonyandjoy.co.uk

I now found myself with multiple therapies under my belt which I had never anticipated. This was all self-development for me, but I loved the fact I was now able to share all three with members of the public. My reiki, crystals and chi machine were now able to help so many people as they also helped me. I found friends and family would pay me extra visits to use them. I got to know many people's stories and had them all leaving with smiles on their faces. Life was good, and I loved it.

I remember taking a couple to a Body and Soul fair in Edinburgh. One of the stall holders kept coming across to where I had people lying on the floor. During a break he advised me that I should have a video playing above. When I asked him why he said that every time the machine switched off, he had to race across to see the look on people's faces! When the machines stop, people get a burst of energy going up their body.

I always remember a person that was in my house trying one out. He said, "Who needs drugs when you can feel like that!" I looked at him as he quickly added "Of course I don't do drugs." I even had a client visit me with her husband. She said to me "Tell him what time you go to bed and how many hours you sleep". I told him 12am till 6am and that I had to force myself to bed, knowing I had work a few hours later. She then said that she had advised her husband that she had never seen someone with so much energy!

MASTER / TEACHER TRAINING

The thing about reiki is it has a mind of its own. I say it chose me and sends me in the direction it wants me to go. After a time, I kept getting a feeling more was to happen. It was like someone kept knocking at my door. I discussed this with my reiki teacher, and he asked me if I would like to go to the next level. I said I was not sure as it was too much money and I could never afford this. Also, I thought I would have no use for the next level. He suggested we put a date in the diary, for almost a year away, and if it was meant to happen, I would have the money before the date. I agreed to this while at the back of my mind thinking it would not happen due to lack of money, so unlike the earlier reiki training, I was not building my hopes up. Also, I thought the next level of training was only for training others. How wrong I was, and synchronicity kicked in again.

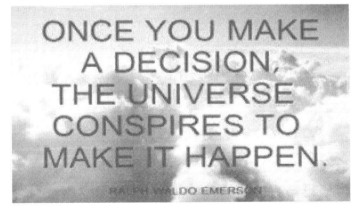

ONCE YOU MAKE A DECISION, THE UNIVERSE CONSPIRES TO MAKE IT HAPPEN.

RALPH WALDO EMERSON

By this time, I had become a distributor for the Sun Ancon Chi machine to spread the word and had already sold a couple, so I put the commission money into an account to add to what I had already saved. I then got money for Christmas again but was about £39 short of the full amount that I needed for the workshop and had no idea where this would come from. Now this may not seem a lot of money to you but back then it was for me. I then got the worst bonus from work that I had ever had. You guessed it- £39. I was on my way. This was my way of knowing that I was taking the right direction in my life. I always said that if you went to the next level that you would make reiki your life and I was not wrong.

The time arrived for my long weekend of training and I went with my teacher David to a lovely cottage in a very quiet village in Scotland for one to one training. While we were on our way, he asked me why was I doing this training? Was it to make money? I advised that I felt it was something I needed to do for me and my family. He was pleased that I did not want to use it in a monetary way. He asked if I would want to train people in reiki and then I uttered words I will never forget. I said I had promised to train my daughter only and no one else. After laughing his words were "Watch this space". I should have taken notice. Once again, my life was about to change but always for the better.

There were only another two or three cottages close by and in front of us was the sea. When I looked out into the back garden, I could see partridges wandering around. It was so peaceful and the most perfect place to learn my Usui Master and Teacher qualifications. It made such an impact on me that later I decided this was the way for me to teach also. I would also always work with very small groups or individuals. This has stayed with me and I feel that I have made lots of friends from many of the people I have trained. I believe this is down to giving personal attention rather than being one of a large group.

I have been blessed to have the same teacher for all my levels and learned so much from him. One thing I took from my training was to make sure people knew they could come back to me if they needed any more information as they grew with the energy. If I did not have the answer, I would pass the question to David and would always get the information I needed. I also learned that at each level there is so much for the mind to take in that it is good to have a period between each level. Reiki is a wonderful gift to be added to your life and it should be enjoyed rather than rushed through. It has been shown to me many times that everyone adjusts to the energy differently and some need more time than others between each level. It is for this reason, I do not believe in giving level one and two together.

During the weekend things went at a very easy pace and when we wanted, we would take a walk or give each other reiki. I cannot put into words the effect this time had on me. Up until that weekend I always said I struggled meditating. As part of the weekend, I was asked to do some meditations. During one meditation a very special bird came to me. Since then I have had it on all my business information. People often now call me the Swan lady. I remember after the weekend was over David sent me a link to T Rex's song Ride a White Swan! I certainly felt after that weekend I was flying high.

It often surprises me that people rush through reiki and take part in websites that offer training all over distance. In these days of wanting bargains I always think you get what you pay for. Experience and practise as one to one, for me, wins hands over all the time. I have been shocked to see some distance training being done with no space in between the levels. To say you can become a Reiki Master / Teacher in a weekend really worries me as people than then go out in the public and charge to both give reiki and attune others. Therefore, the UK Reiki Federation will only register you if you have trained in person.

I can understand people wanting to learn to heal themselves as reiki is a fantastic modality but before you go and teach, I strongly believe you need a lot more interaction and practice. How can this be done with no one checking on how you are working? When I think of the students I have trained over the years, some have needed more practice and guidance than others to feel secure in the knowledge that they are doing the right thing. Another thing about distance and especially all the cheap deals out there is that some people may have no back up if they have questions after being trained. These may arise months or even years after training so it's always good to check with any teacher about this before paying out any money.

Another thing you should ask of anyone training you in reiki is to see their Lineage. This shows who trained them, going all the way back to Dr Usui.

DECISION TIME

After this weekend when I grew so much spiritually, my head had quite a bit of sorting out to do. I still thought I would only ever train my daughter but did not know how long it would take before I wanted to do this. I knew that after each level taken by me, I had been affected in different ways, so I was not in any hurry. I knew that I would know when the time was right to train my daughter. For me this was such a big change that I spent the next few months working more on myself until I felt ready to train my daughter. When this day happened, we were both blown away. I think possibly because we had a connection, that the energy on the day I attuned her was like magic. This coupled with when I had done Past Life Ascension with her remain two of my most treasured moments with her. Since then I have trained her to level two, her husband to level one and both her children as well. I love having family that are so connected.

After this, someone I knew asked me to re attune her to level two which I was happy to do, and this then gave me more confidence. When she had been previously attuned, she advised me that the difference between level one and two she had not liked. When she did level two, she could no longer feel the energy flowing. Instead her intuition had increased. This was good as there were a couple of incidents that she received warnings about which enabled her to save both herself and her daughters lives at different times. I explained to her that the more you work with reiki the more the intuition expands and that it had been the right thing for her at that time. After re-attuning her she said she felt much better and the feeling of the energy came back again so she was happier.

Over the next few months, everywhere I went people seemed to be talking about reiki. I remember walking in my local park and a stranger came to me and started to talk about a health problem she had, and could I suggest a reiki therapist as someone had advised her that reiki could help. The final straw for a friend was when we went on a weekend away with the same social group I had started out with, to find a group of people were talking about where to get trained in a town an hour away from me. As I knew someone in that town, I gave them his details. Funnily enough it was the person who had originally been going to train me. My friend reminded me that I could have asked them to come to me for training as I was only a one-hour ride away. I felt that I had done the right thing but took her comments on board. Once we had talked over how much I kept having people speaking to me about reiki I gave in and said I would get a website created and see if anyone contacted me.

I have another friend who used to spend a week with me each summer with her family. When she arrived for her holiday, I advised what I was going to do. Much to my surprise she asked if she could try doing it for me. Lucky me, as she went on to build me my first ever website. This was a practise for her as she had only ever made one website before, but I loved it. Synchronicity had struck again. My swans were incorporated into the website and now I felt I had a presence on the internet. She had also made use of colour to make sure anyone with visual problems could see the website easier. The rest as they say is history. Within one week I had someone contact me to be trained in reiki one and another for reiki two. As my teacher had said, you are led in the direction you need to take with reiki. It is a living energy and always looks out for your highest and greatest good.

This was a good learning curve for me. I sat down and structured how my training days would unfold and felt ready for whoever was to come my way. My teacher had said that his manuals were to be shared so I had these to start me off but over time have made my own ones.

I thought about the training from when I used to train people to see if they wanted to become childminders. During that time, I would see around 100 people over a few nights and usually by the end of the information evenings there may only be 25% or less of people left but they were committed to going forward in that line of work. I always remember doing a role play with a group. I asked what they would do in a certain situation. One ladies answer was "I would smack him across the face!" You can guess that she was not destined to become a childminder. Now I had the opportunity to take people that were 100% committed from day one to change their lives with the help of reiki. I felt almost ready but still a bit scared of running a workshop on my own for the first time.

During this time, I was a member of a website called Just for the love of it. This was set up by a man who wanted to change the world by getting people to help others without expecting anything in return. I remember sharing the info on a money saving website. The next I heard from Mark was to say they had contacted him to check his servers were not crashing! He was getting thousands of people signing up through my link on the site. Check out his book called The Moneyless Man as he went on to live over a year without using money.

Someone contacted me via the Free Economy (This was another name for it) to have a coffee and chat. She wanted advice on learning reiki, so I offered this to her. At the end of our chat she said she wanted to be trained by me. She advised me that she knew another teacher but for various reasons did not want to be taught by her. I was shocked but thought this would be a good way to try out my reiki teaching skills. The night before she called to ask if she could bring beetroot soup and bread- both homemade- for our lunch. After the day had finished, I realised I had not spoken of any money for this training, after all I had given her a whole day of my time. When I started out, I thought I was giving a couple of hours of my time to have coffee and a chat! When I looked back on it, I realised we both received what we had required from the day. I now no longer had any fear of teaching members of the public and she was now able to use reiki on herself. I loved how Synchronicity had played a part in this too. It was also a good learning curve, not to put a time on how much we can help other people.

I always love when I meet up with students four weeks after training to see what their experiences have been both for themselves and with others. Clients are always advised for twenty-one days they go through a cleansing period and sometimes things that they have hidden away in the past come back into their minds. The good thing is the reiki energy helps them to overcome whatever problems surface, so they can move on with their life without the past impacting on them. Many times, they experience a feeling of joy as if a weight has been lifted off their shoulders. After attunement, colours can feel deeper and brighter and often people feel more in touch with nature. This is one of the biggest impacts it has had on me. After my training, I found myself wanting to spend more time in my local parks and by the sea. I now find it easy to block out all sounds around me and just listen to the birds. The colours of the flowers seem to jump out at me as well. I usually do some energy work first thing in the morning when it is peaceful. Funnily enough, When I was at work, I had headphones on and often missed out on being told to stop taking calls. I think this is because I learned to switch off and focus on just one thing. People used to laugh at me when they found I was still taking calls after 30 minutes after they had stopped.

I remember another thing happening at work. I had a Manager

who used to laugh at me as she didn't understand energy work. During team time each Friday we would all get together, and she would ask what we were doing at the weekend. People would be going to the pubs and concerts and other things. One day she was passing us to another manager as she was going on holiday and said, "Joy will give you a laugh". This was because the previous weekend I had gone to both a Spiritualist church and seen a Physic Surgeon which had half of my team laughing on the floor when they heard this. Around that time, I had been asked to do an interview with author Faith Canter. When my manager returned from her holiday she asked if I had done the interview and could she listen to it? That surprised me, especially as she immediately went and got her headphones on. About thirty minutes later she came over and apologised to me as she had never understood what I did, and now had a better understanding. I always say that all that is required is for people to be open to things they don't understand.

MASSIVE SYNCHRONICITY

A few years down the line I had a foreign language student staying with me. As I wanted to add some things to my website, and I had forgotten how to do what was required, I asked his advice. He was a web design student, so when he said he asked if as part of his studies, he could redesign it, I took him up on his offer. The only problem with this was he went back home to France without telling me how to get into my website or change things myself. I was not so happy with my site after his changes and determined to learn how to do this myself which was to take time. I decided to do a night class at my local college so that if I got someone to redesign my website, I would then be able to keep it up to date by understanding what I was doing.

At college, I learned that he had changed the operating system of my website, but only some of it. This meant it was more messed up than I had been aware of. The Lecturer was shocked that my website was still working. I knew to get a new website made was going to cost me a lot of money that I did not have. The alternate was one of the cheap ones which looked very unprofessional at that time. I found the course interesting but was then in over my head after a few weeks when the lecturer concentrated on teaching Dreamweaver. At that point he lost me. I was feeling disheartened with my course and wondering what I should do moving forward. Around this time a massive piece of synchronicity happened. I had a call from my son who worked inside a web design company. He advised me that he had someone willing to make me a website for free as he already had a template for a similar one. I was so pleased to feel that soon I would be the happy owner of a professional well-designed website that of course I said yes. I got a lot more than I thought and ended up with my fantastic website.

The fabulous thing was my website was designed by the person who had created the original template. He was also good at optimising websites so that they could be found. The only cost to me was a reiki treatment for his wife and I added in a pregnancy massage from my friend for her also. The universe was really helping me to move forward. After this I had therapists in other countries contacting me to say what they thought of my website. People who knew me said it was just right for me. This person, for quite a while after, even helped maintain my website while teaching my son how to do the job also. To this day I call upon my son when I need help although he has advised me, I need to check YouTube first for any answers. It's amazing what you can find on that site.

I decided that to go with my super new website I needed special business cards. When I had been out with my dog, I came across a bench in memory of someone and the words resonated with me. Every time I passed, I had to read them as I kept feeling a pull towards them. I later learned they were written by Ralph Waldo Emerson. "Do not go where the path may lead, go instead where there is no path and leave a trail."

I really felt as if I was started on a new journey, a new way of life. I wanted to do it my way and felt that many changes were coming.

SYNCHRONICITY RULES!

I owe the way I run my workshops to my teacher. At the time he taught me, he always had very small groups of people in his workshops. This made it a very informal enjoyable way of learning. I am happy to teach someone reiki as an individual or in very small groups - usually no more than eight. I feel it is a joyous thing to learn and the day should be taken at the pace that is right for the individuals. During one period synchronicity played a big part in my reiki workshops.

I received a call for someone wishing to book a reiki session. This person had Myalgic Encephalopathy (M.E.). The next week my friend who also had M.E asked for the same. A couple of weeks later I had someone with M.E asking to use the chi machine. Do you think the universe was trying to tell me something? This is when something happened that blew me away. A local M.E charity contacted me to say they had been given a grant to train people in different types of therapies, so they would be able to help others with this illness. They asked if I would like to train two people. The interesting thing was none of the many people that were going to be trained knew which therapy they were to be trained in.

I advised that reiki was different in that it affects you both mentally and spiritually in many ways and people should be aware of this if they wanted to take part. She did advise that a previous person had decided after level one training not to go on to the next level. I said that I would want to make sure that the people chosen knew how they may be affected as it was not like massage when you could just learn the strokes. (No disrespect to massage therapists intended). With reiki, the mind / spirit is involved also. She then advised me she would be giving the students the contact telephone numbers of four other reiki teachers and would advise them to decide, after speaking to them all, who they wanted to be trained by.

A week later I had just come home at lunchtime when the first person called me, and we spoke for a while. A few days later I had just come home for a short while later in the afternoon when the second person called me, and again we spoke for some time. Later I was talking to a friend and I advised I knew the students were going to choose me. When she asked how I knew, I said that there was only one hour out of each of those days at different times when I was at home, and they both called during that time. Sure enough, they each called back with an affirmative to be trained by me. One of them called while I was talking to a group of people about synchronicity and about all my M.E experiences! The next bit of synchronicity was when they met outside my home and found that they both knew each other. What a brilliant start to the day.

We had arranged a training day starting a bit later in the day and allowed their health to dictate the speed of the training. I found I was much more tired than usual at the end of the day as the pace was quite slow. Over the next few days both contacted me to go over little bits as the memories of people that have M.E are often impaired. This is where only teaching small groups comes into its own. It means that I have time for people who need extra help and support. A few months later they came back for level two training. As this was over a couple of days, I had to completely change how I actioned my training that weekend. At the end of it and after they had done their homework over the next four weeks, I was pleased to have two reiki practitioners now ready to help their charity. The special point of reiki level two was to enable them to send distance reiki when someone with M.E was too ill to receive a visit. One of them called me a couple of weeks later to advise he had just had a massive coincidence. He had gone to a shopping centre and was going around and around in circles looking for a parking space. Out of the corner of his eye he saw a space become available, so he drove in to it. When he got out of his car, he was astounded to see the car next to him had the number plate Joy so told me I must have been watching out for him. He also said when I was writing my story, I had to add his story into it, so this is for you Jeff Begg. Unfortunately, Jeff passed away before I got this book published.

Most of the time I can accept whatever life gives me but if I struggle at any point I can go and meditate for a while and give myself reiki and it all comes back into perspective again. Reiki is a tool that is with me whenever I need it. The thing I am most pleased about though is how relaxed and chilled out I feel. I now have a much more positive attitude to everything, which has enabled me to write articles about this very subject. You can check out some of these at my website: https://peaceharmonyandjoy.co.uk/category/blog/ I'll say it again and again - "I love reiki".

ORBS

One summer I was asked for a photo of me working for a charity newsletter. As I was hosting foreign language students one said he would take some photographs for me, so I went and got my neighbour to come through to my house. We tried posing with the therapy table in different areas of the room trying to get good snaps while having quite a few giggles in the process. At one point I felt the energy kick in and she did also. I remember her telling me I was not meant to be treating her at that time, so we had a laugh. It just shows that the energy can decide when to make an appearance without being invited. The interesting thing is when the photographs were uploaded to my computer there were orbs in the ones at exactly the points where we felt the energy kick in. When I uploaded this photo to Face book it was pointed out that there was also another orb there too.

Orbs are nothing new in my house. I had my last dog Misty until she was almost 12 years of age. During this time, she would often stare into the air as if she could see something I could not. It used to freak out some visitors although regulars would just say "She's at it again!" This was before I really knew about spiritual orbs but on looking back at photographs of her, she was often surrounded by them. I remember two friends dog sitting for me and they took a photograph of Misty. Sure enough, there were orbs around her. They wanted to know if she had brought them to their house. Animals can be very spiritual and intuitive. Misty sure was and is still around me today.

I remember going to a place near Edinburgh called Rosslyn Chapel with other people that I met. A lot of people connect Rosslyn with the Knights Templar. We had all been on David's Facebook page as he had trained us all at different times. Two of them, who I had never met before, invited me the next day to the Chapel. They decided to visit a cave situated below the Chapel and asked if I wished to go there too. That was a day of experiences. When we went to the road, we found it blocked off with large metal gates. There was a very small space between the edge of the gate and the road. One of them pulled out a space blanket and laid it on the ground under the gate. We then, with a bit of trepidation, all crawled underneath it. On the way to the cave we stopped at a tree. One of the ladies explained it was so twisted due to a vortex. At this point she brought out divining rods and crystal pendulums. It was interesting to see them all at work. When we got to the cave it was so dark that I could not see inside it. One of the ladies gave me a singing bowl. I was astonished to see that while I used it, the cave was brighter, and I could see right to the back of it. As soon as I stopped, it went dark again. Both ladies felt the presence of spirits while they were inside. We had taken a few photographs and found, when they were uploaded to a computer, that there were Orbs exactly at the points they both felt Spirits!

I remember after that that we decided to go for a meal at a hotel near bye. I was walking towards it still trying to get the mud off my clothes! That was a day of experiences for me that will forever stay in my memory.

LEARNING CONTINUES

One of the things I have learned through reiki is that everything happens for a reason. I always look for a positive outcome in every situation. If I cannot see one at that time, I know that I will get the answer in the future, as many times things happen now to affect the future rather than the present. A teacher never stops learning and growing. One does not stay static. I have learned this both through my clients and taking extra workshops with other professionals. It is important to keep the brain active and continue to learn.

Often people start with Usui reiki and then learn more. One of the most important points I believe is to be trained in person and to see the lineage of who is teaching you. Through the family tree, everyone should link back to Dr Usui. I am also a member of the UK Reiki Federation. They are currently trying to get reiki seen as a professional holistic practice in the same way as massage is. They also expect people to learn through continuing with their personal development. This is a good thing, as in all walks of life people are trained in their job and years later refuse to move with the times. Take computers for example. Some people believe these are alien to them and would rather give up work than learn something new. Working with energy makes you meet so many people who can have an impact on your learning as it has done for me. I have met many fantastic people over the last few years and been introduced to so much by them, that I am learning more all the time.

I never thought I would want to learn another form of reiki but found myself looking, through Social Media at Karuna reiki. This is open to people who have already reached the Usui master level and during it you learn extra symbols. This was brought about by William Lee Rand who found that sometimes extra symbols came into his head while he was working with the energy. When he spoke to other master's they said the same thing had happened to some of them. They then decided to take all the symbols collectively and use them and then report back on which ones they found more effective. After this Karuna reiki was born.

I was drawn to a website and was pleased to note that they allowed a learning grant to be used but then noted it was for the other therapies taught, not Karuna. I decided that it was not time for me to learn as I knew it would be this person who would train me, and I was willing to wait. I put out my intention that if it was correct for me to be trained in this therapy that it would happen. I checked the website every few weeks as I kept being pulled back to it. On one of these visits I was pleased to see that I could now use my grant for the training to take place, so I was over the moon.

SAYING GOODBYE TO MISTY

The only thing to mar this time was my wonderful dog Misty was going to be put to sleep on the day after my workshop took place. This was due to a tumour that was discovered a few days before that was inoperable. My family insisted that I went on the training as I had wanted to do it for such a long time, and they wanted the time with my dog Misty. I agreed that my family could keep her while I was on the training. This was to allow my grandchildren the time to say goodbye to her and have lots of cuddles. At this point she was in no pain and was still eating and drinking and looked like nothing was wrong with her. I took her to my daughters the night before my course started. The next day I was called to say that she had deteriorated suddenly, and we agreed for her to be taken to the vets that day. As I had already said my goodbye to her the night before, it was agreed that my daughter would take her. I felt very confused as to whether I should continue with my course but in the end made the decision to carry on with it. During the day of the course we all sent our love to Misty. The interesting thing for my daughter was she had previously needed to put one of her dogs to sleep. This had been a traumatic experience for her as it took many people to hold the dog still. She advised me that Misty's passing was a very peaceful experience with the vet giving her treats while she was being cuddled by my daughter and of course the grandchildren had spoiled her beforehand with lots of the same. It gave my daughter a better ending to remember Misty's passing when thinking of being at a vet's surgery. So, on this occasion synchronicity had stepped in when it was required.

One interesting fact here was that Misty, as well as my previous dog Kyla, both made their presence known after they passed over. Kyla was heard going up and down the stairs in the evening for a few days. Misty, I felt beside me on a couple of occasions. Around this time, I made friends with an Animal Communicator in Canada on social media and found it interesting that we could contact animals both in the present and after they had passed over. I also found that a lot of people that communicated with animals also practised reiki. This was to later take me down a different path which again was through synchronicity.

I remember Misty had always moved away from me when I went to give her reiki. This is when I learned animals are just like us and can choose whether they require reiki or not. The day after my master /teacher training I came home, and she sat on my lap and the energy switched on. To my surprise she stayed their letting the reiki flow through her. I wonder if she thought before that I was not good enough for her. A short time after, she was standing beside me on my settee when I saw that she lost control of her legs. She started shaking uncontrollably and I found myself panicking. After a few seconds I had a light bulb moment and started the reiki flowing. Within a couple of minutes, she had stopped shaking and managed to sit down.

The following week the same thing happened when she was in my garden. At least this time I knew to go straight to giving her reiki. It worked very quickly, and I had arranged a visit to the vet soon after. We found that her Cruciate Ligament needed operated on. I used reiki a lot on her during the recovery period. She was very happy to receive the reiki from me. Perhaps she knew in advance that she would require this help when she first accepted reiki from me. On her last day with me, I made sure she received lots of reiki, but was unaware that this would be the last time I would see her.

Is Reiki Crazy? Think Again!

One of the things I am finding is that there appears to be a shift in many of the people coming to see me for reiki. At one point I saw two educational psychologists at separate times. They did not know each other but advised me that many educational staff around them were going on spiritual retreats. They were also learning meditation to teach the children in their classes. I am also seeing more people who have scientific backgrounds. To them reiki is something they cannot explain but as they feel so much better after receiving it, I tell them not to stress thinking about why. A reiki student advised me that in this day of technology it was great to find something so natural that helped in such a positive way.

I am also finding more and more people are opening to reiki. I remember when I first started out everyone thought I was crazy. No one believed in it. Now there have been so many studies done with placebo groups that there is more proof out there, which I am so happy to hear. I remember when I had my level one workshop everyone was given a copy of an experiment done in a hospital environment using a machine that they were both wired up to. It showed one person giving and another receiving reiki. The person giving reiki had a higher vibration than the one receiving it. The interesting thing that happened though, was the person receiving the energy found his vibrations increased until they were on a par with the higher one. This has always stuck with me. So now the scientists are being able to decipher why reiki works but we still have a long way to go.

Reiki is very easy to learn. It is activated by intention from a reiki teacher who is attuned to the energy. Once attuned you may choose to join a group for support and on-going personal development. Many teachers will have group sessions to let people come together and share treatments. It also gives you the opportunity to ask questions. Of course, you should also have your reiki teacher available to you as well. Don't think by looking at symbols online that you will learn. Some of the original teachers of reiki did not write anything down. This means that when they went on to teach others the symbols may not have been the same as they were taught. This is the reason you will see many different looking symbols online for the same name. This does not matter though as the way a teacher attunes is correct for you as an individual.

Reiki should be integrated into your life. Once attuned, it is there for you to use without limits. Use it every day both on yourself and things around you. If I'm ever feeling I need a bit TLC I give myself reiki to raise me back up again. This is not to say that I do not get outside help as well. Therapists can be so focussed on helping others that they can forget about themselves. I am lucky to have people that I can swap a treatment with so we each help each other. It is also said that there should always be an exchange with reiki. This may mean money, a cup of coffee or help in another way. To be able to have exchanges with therapists is an ideal way to share.

SOCIAL MEDIA

The advent of Social media platforms such as Face book, Twitter and LinkedIn have speeded up my connections to other people, especially reiki masters in other countries. The bonds stretch worldwide. It also means we can all come together and send distant healing if anyone or anywhere in the world requires it. I have met, both online and in person, some wonderful people who all work in the energy field and they fill my life with such positive vibrations. There is such a lot of positivity out there. All you need do is align yourself to it. Of course, we are all human and sometimes things can get us down but having reiki at hand can certainly help you through problems. Because of the friends that I have made worldwide on the social media platforms, I find that at different times of the day I get lots of positive quotes and pictures coming into my news feeds. I love this type of sharing and I often add in my own experiences. I remember one time being asked to befriend a reiki master in another country. She felt isolated as people did not respect reiki due to their religion even though reiki has nothing at all to with this. Many of us befriended her and she has now turned things around and has a successful practice. Often when we see world events such as disasters taking place, we can all arrange online a time, irrespective of where we are to come together. It may even be for a whole day so that at different times people in each country will be sending the energy out. With reiki, you never need to feel powerless. Energy, even from one person is strong. I remember reading about Washington in America where hundreds of people sat in the city centre and meditated. Crime rate dropped by about 23%! Imagine that same energy going out to disaster areas.

Social media can be used for good or otherwise. I feel it is important to connect with the right type of people online. I have done webinars and connected, through friends, with people that have all helped me on the journey I am on. It is not a place to have arguments and fall out with people. If you find this is happening often to you, I would suggest taking a step back and see if these people are right for you at this time. Sometimes people can also get lost in social media and forget to have a life outside of it. Don't let it take over your life. Life really is for living, not just existing.

MY NEW PUPPIES

Misty had died in October 2012 and the following January I went with my daughter to a workshop on happiness. During this we were asked to think about how we woke up when the alarm clock went off. Was it a "HELLO WORLD!" or was it a case of pushing the snooze button and not wanting to get out of bed? I realised that before Misty had died, I would have jumped out of the bed immediately, and as soon as I was dressed, would be out walking the dog. After she died, I was in no hurry to get out of bed as all I needed to do was get dressed and go to work. This workshop was wakeup call in more than one way. I decided before I left that I was going to get another dog, but it had to be one that liked children, dogs, cats and being able to be at home alone for a few hours. Not a lot to ask for lol. I spoke with The Scottish Springer Spaniel Rescue who did a home assessment but advised I could wait a while for the ideal dog to become available.

I decided to visit my local cat and Dog Home which was full of Staffordshire Bull Terriers and those crossed with the breed. As my dog was to spend an amount of time at my daughters' home, she had said no Staffies were allowed. Guess what type of dog she bought a year later? You've guessed right if you said Staffie cross. They are a very lovable breed and great for families. In fact, their nickname is "The Nanny dog". Now by this time I did not want to wait for a dog and found myself logging in to Gumtree and looking at the dogs for sale adverts. As I would not have trusted what people said from rehoming an older dog I decided on a puppy. I have to say I had done my research before this and knew what pitfalls to watch out for. Here is where synchronicity came up again.

A few days later a new advert appeared for puppies and I fell in love with one. I do not know where my thoughts came from, but I found myself emailing to apply to rehome two! The owner replied saying there was one only left so I arranged with my daughter to visit the next day as she lived closer and I was working. Unknown to me my daughter the next day called the owner who asked why I wanted two. My daughter said that as I had previously had one, I always wondered if two would be better for company. At that point the person advised she was going to keep one herself but if I visited with my daughter that night, she would have decided whether to keep it.

When we arrived to see the four-week-old pups she handed one to me and advised it was the one I had fallen in love with in the photo posted on line. She then said to pick another. My daughter picked the second pup. I was overjoyed at being given two. Now the hard work was to start.

After I went home, I knew I had four weeks to arrange day care cover but, in my head, I did not want a professional dog walker. I put it out there that I would rather have a dog lover who was unable to keep a dog their self. To this end I put an advert in the local post office in my street. Then the biggest surprise happened. Someone answered my advert and advised not only had we met at the Happiness workshop but also that she lived in my street and knew just the person to help. Talk about Synchronicity, and it did not stop there. She introduced me to her neighbour Jinty who took in elderly rescue dogs and was currently awaiting one. She advised she could spend eight weeks with my dogs till they were allowed outside after their inoculations. Instead, when she finally received a dog it was so poorly it could not walk much at all due to the sores on its feet. This meant she stayed on and walked my dogs every day for me for over a year. Remember earlier I told you about all the people with M.E contacting me? This lady had both M.E and Fibromyalgia. After a year we got someone she knew to help her out for the next year until the person took over fully.

I was determined when I got my new puppies, that I would get them used to reiki. They accepted a small amount from me at first, so I gradually built it up. When they were about eight months old, they were both attacked by another dog. This caused them afterwards to react to noises. It could be as simple as someone closing a door to their car outside. With Firework night coming up I decided to play sounds of fireworks going off at the same time as giving them reiki. It worked so well that they both fell asleep while all the bangs were taking place. Since then I can take them outside during fireworks going off and they do not bother at all. I had a laugh one day when I was running a reiki workshop. One of my students was in love with one of my dogs that she was sitting cuddling, when she jumped and said "The reiki has switched on. What do I do?" I asked her to keep her hands on my dog, so we could build up the time that she allowed reiki to be given. Now I find both dogs often let my students practise on them. In the beginning they would not allow me to send distance reiki in their presence. Perhaps it was too strong for them and they would always interrupt me to make it stop. Thankfully they are happy to stay beside me now when myself and students send reiki. By practising distance reiki on the dogs, before people, the students get to see when the dog decides it has had enough energy. They usually find that at the same time the dog moves that the energy has stopped.

ANIMAL COMMUNICATION

During this time, I had been watching all the feedback the Animal Communicator in Canada was getting from people. This sparked an interest in me to do this as well when she advised anyone could learn this. I decided I wanted to explore this myself but as I had never heard of this before speaking to her, I wondered how I could learn from such a distance and wondered if there was anywhere in Scotland I could go to learn. The next week after making this decision I was checking for updates on a therapists' group on Facebook and someone came on asking if anyone would like to go to her place of business and give reiki to horses. This was a big step up from dogs, but I immediately signed up for it. Although it was not communicating in the way I wanted, I thought it would be great to be able to see how horses responded to reiki. It was not the right time for me though as my back went the day before I had the long drive to get there. A few weeks later, on speaking to someone that had been there I was told of the amazing things that happened when they sent distance reiki across the fields to the horses. They had been advised that when they were told to stop, that they should do so immediately as one of the horses could play up. They started sending reiki and all the horses turned and started walking towards the therapists. Suddenly a very large one started racing towards them and the owner told them all to stop sending reiki. As soon as they stopped, all the animals immediately stopped walking and running, and turned away from them then went further back into the field. It sounded like an awesome experience, but I knew my time would come. A few months later

I decided to go to a Meet Up group run by someone I know. There was only one other person there apart from the organiser. I remember thinking why am I here? At one point he played a meditation CD and advised that this was from an Animal Communicator in Scotland!

Talk about synchronicity and she only lived over the bridge from me so often came to Edinburgh to teach. When he told me that he had been learning from her, I went home and immediately bought her book on Kindle. That day I signed up to do a course with her.

The course was over two days and during the first day we had three dogs pay us a visit. I fell in love with a spaniel that was blind. It was amazing the information we were able to get from the dog. I was hooked! I remember asking what his favourite thing was and the word FISH was shown to me in large capital letters. I remember thinking "Why would I make this up" as surely a dog would not have this as a favourite thing? The owner burst out laughing and advised me that when he returned home from fishing, the dog could check out and smell any caught fish and loved this. The other thing was asking what the dog disliked and I got shown the word CAT. My thoughts were that of course most dogs did not like cats, so thought nothing of this, till the other people at the workshop had the same experience. The owner advised he had rehomed the dog the year before because he had been mistreated which had caused his blindness, but he had never got on with their cat and they each kept to a different floor of the house. In fact, this was the real reason he had brought the dog to the workshop. After this day he decided to stop trying to get them to interact with each other as the other people at the workshop gave him some further information. The dog was grateful for being rescued by the family but had advised that the cat thought he had a right to be there. That did not sit well with the dog. He thought the cat should also be thanking the owners. I think we all know a cat that rules the roost and expects everyone to pander to him. This was that cat.

The second day we did distance work which really did not seem weird as I was used to sending distance reiki to people, so this was just another step up. During this time each of us got the opportunity to connect distantly with other animals whether they were still alive or had passed over. I had a good connection with one dog and found out so much information from him. This was corroborated by the others taking part and the owner who was running the course. It was so amazing to be able to connect in this way to animals. Someone connected to one of my dogs which was an interesting experience for me. I had taken in a photograph of my two dogs. She asked permission to cover the male as she said he wanted to speak on behalf of his sister! After giving it, she said my female dog wanted to help with therapies.

Synchronicity then struck again when the next week I was on Facebook and someone posted that they were looking for more therapy pets to go into hospitals, homes and prisons, so I went to sign her and brother Merlin up for this. When the paperwork arrived, I found that one of the things the dogs should not do is react to noises, I knew at this time it was not for them. The interesting thing was at that time whenever I had clients upstairs in my therapy room, Willow would always bark so I often had to leave her with a friend. When I asked the person, who had connected to her, she advised my dog wanted to see where I worked from. She even said if she was not allowed to walk upstairs that I could carry her, and she would be happy at this. As my dogs were never allowed upstairs, I did as she requested and since then she has been quiet when I have clients! Imagine being able to talk to animals! It was amazing, knowing that we do have the means of listening to our pets. The only thing that spooked me a little was speaking to a cat that had passed over.

After my Animal communication workshop, I had won for the trainer to speak with one of my dogs. Their antics are poles apart. Willow has a very frenetic energy and Merlin is much calmer. Merlin had not been much of a cuddler and always had a sad look in his eyes. She told me he felt responsible for his sister and had knowledge of problems in his past lives. She advised him that it was my job to look after both and he had to let go of the responsibility of looking after his sister. He told her he didn't think he could do that. I told her I was going to attune Willow to reiki to see if it calmed her down, and did she think it would be helpful for Merlin. She burst out laughing. When I asked her why, she told me Merlin's words were" I thought she would never ask!" The very next day I attuned him, and the sad eyes disappeared.

I found out so much in that chat with her. I found my previous dog Misty had been chatting to Merlin from Spirit and giving him advice. Something funny happened during that communication. She had called to say she had been speaking to Merlin over distance but need an extra 10 minutes with him. Merlin then told her it was okay to continue while on the phone with me. She told me that when on the phone she could also pick up other animals. As Willow was there, she was brought into the conversation. I asked them why they had eaten my settee and got the response they were too excited, and it had smelled nice! At one point the trainer said Willow was putting her hands over her ears to say she was not listening. At that point, to my surprise, Willow got up and went in the garden. This is something she never did on her own. She obviously did not like getting a row.

I decided it was time to try to communicate myself with Merlin for the first time after that. The first time I told him without speaking that I had a treat in my pocket for him. He came over to me and went straight to where the treat was. Fired up by this, a couple of days later I again communicated with him and said that

I really missed not getting cuddles from him and that I would love for this to change. He came over to me and put his head on my chest and stayed there giving me a massive cuddle. This has continued to this day. Whenever I come home or come downstairs in the morning, he immediately puts his head on my chest to get a hug. For anyone that does not believe in Animal communication, I can only say that it has been proved time and again to me.

His sister Willow is the complete opposite and loves cuddles. Now she must sometimes push Merlin out of the way which I find funny. There is nothing more wonderful than cuddling up to two dogs which is what happens often now. Merlin can look at you with such serious eyes or happy eyes. I very occasionally see sad eyes but as they are not there for long, they don't worry me. It's such a special thing to know that not only do animals want to be understood, they also want you to communicate with them. I feel so grateful to have these animals in my life.

THE CELESTINE PROPHECY

I remember years ago a friend speaking to me and saying that she had a book that I must read. She advised when she came over for a holiday, she would bring it with her. The next week I was surprised to get post from her with a note that it was meant to be read by me now, not in a few months. The book was The Celestine Prophecy by James Redfield. That was my introduction to understanding synchronicity. I shared this book with friends, and it made an impact on them too. It also introduced me to the different types of people among us and I saw myself back then as a "poor me". As soon as I realised this, I started to make changes in my life. I then went on Amazon and bought the remaining books in the series but was to get a surprise. The next day I received an email to advise me that Amazon were sorry, but they were out of one of the books. The same day one of the friends that I had passed the book onto contacted me to say she had bought another book by James Redfield. Yes, you've guessed it; this was the one I had missed out on. The interesting thing though was she did not buy it from Amazon!

When I read the next book, I struggled with it but did complete it. Whereas the Celestine Prophecy had flowed, the second book felt made up. I know this sounds funny, but the first book gelled with me so much I felt the author was speaking from experience. I decided not to follow it through to read the other books at that time so left them in my bookcase.

A couple of years later someone I know asked if I had read the last book in the series. I told him why I was not reading them, and he said everything in the book was true. He also said that after my birthday I was to speak to him as he had a numerology message for me. My birthday came and went, and I then remembered that I needed to contact him. On the same day I picked up my SPICE Scotland magazine to see what events I would like to take part in. Surprise, surprise he was doing a workshop soon after. I called the office and offered to coordinate the workshop for them which was accepted - the synchronicity was ongoing.

That night I was about to get into my bed when a book fell from the book case and landed on my floor at my feet. Thank goodness it didn't land on my feet as it was heavy! After looking at it and realising that this was the book my friend said I really needed to read, I must admit I was more than a little spooked. That night and on the following few nights I stepped over the book rather than picking it up! Eventually I picked it up and decided to see if the time was right for me to read this book. I was amazed that everything made sense and I loved reading it.

The next week I went to my friend's workshop and the first thing he shouted out as I came through the door to the room was "You've read THE BOOK. You've read THE BOOK!" When I asked why he knew this, he said my aura was so wide and held his hands and arms apart as far as they could go. I realised that the only thing that had changed from when I had been going to read the book before was that I had become a reiki master, so obviously I was not ready for it previously. The saying that "Things will come at the right time for you" was so true in this instance. For those of you that have not read the first book – also called The Ninth In-sight – people say that you should not buy it for yourself. Instead it should be given as a gift to you.

I am grateful that my friend started me on this journey, but the synchronicity did not end there. A few years later I was checking my Twitter feeds and saw I had a new follower. It was James Redfield and even more interesting was on his page a photo of his brand-new book The Twelfth Insight. Guess who got in the car and went immediately to the bookshop? One hour later I was reading his new book which I really enjoyed. Social media really does help getting information out to people.

YOUR THOUGHTS
REALLY DO MATTER

Reiki is energy and so are your thoughts. Have you heard of the Law of Attraction or the Secret? It is all about putting your thoughts out to the universe and believing they have been actioned. A friend and I were speaking a few years ago about her business. She had previously had a quiet year due to working on her house and decided that now she was ready to have her business booming. We spoke about imagining it as if it had already happened. She put it out that she would have fifty new clients in the next year. As a wedding planner this was a lot more than she usually actioned due to her daughter.

Less than five months into the year after our chat she had not only exceeded her target she also had clients for the following year as well. She had also worried about her business taking her away from the local area as her daughter was still in school. I said if you put that out there too help will come. Just as her business took off, my shifts changed at work. The only day she was stuck for childcare was one Thursday to pick up her daughter from school. Guess who was given a Thursday off as part of her new shift? Me! She now travels all over Scotland with her business and has even got a new business partner in the catering side. She has also won many awards including Scotland Wedding planner of the year as well as United Kingdom and Ireland Wedding Planner of the Year! I can't believe how far Roni has come. I love the way things work out. I have also trained her in reiki, so she has the way to keep herself calm for all the families and businesses she works with.

One day we were chatting about how well things had worked out for her and she asked what my intentions were for the future. I started saying that I required a certain amount of money to clear my way forward. She advised me that the Secret website had cheques you could download for yourself. I did this and filled it in with the figure I had mentioned and tucked it into my purse. A couple of days later I received a letter to say my credit card limit had increased by a massive amount. As I was planning on transferring to a zero-interest rate card I ignored this. I went ahead and signed for the new card but had no idea how much credit they would give. When it arrived, I was blown away by how much credit it offered. Now you can see why so many people get into debt. To my amazement when I added the two credit cards together, they exceeded the amount on the cheque in my purse by £2000. I laughed thinking I had obviously forgotten to say I did not want to pay it back again. My thoughts had been worked on very quickly though.

Months later I decided to try the same to see what would happen. This time I said I wanted x amount of money but did NOT want to have to pay it back. Around this time the UK government advised if you had a private pension that you could access it early as they had changed the pension rules. I only knew of two pensions I had. I paid a tiny amount into one while I had been married, always expecting to have my husband's larger pension to support us. I also worked for the Civil Service for a few years, so I wrote to both companies expecting a very small amount of equity. Imagine my surprise when I found I was due more than expected, plus I found another tiny one. With these I more than made the amount I had wanted plus I did not need to pay it back.

I then put it out that I wanted an additional stream of income. I had no idea what I was looking for until I saw someone I know in

Spain mentioning a product. I checked to see if I could get it in the UK and ordered a sample from Amazon. To say that I was pleased at the difference this product made to my face would be an understatement. I sent a photo to a friend and she asked me to walk down to her house, so she could see it in person. I had my thoughts about the changes confirmed by her.

At this point all I wanted was to acquire more of this product so checked out if anyone was selling it direct from the UK and found someone. I contacted her and found this was a business that I could become involved with. I was pleased that I found something that I believed would fly out the door. Now that I knew it was a business, I decided to contact the person in Spain. She gave me the contact info for someone in her team that was in the UK and we arranged to Skype. I found that this person was a top seller and would be able to give me tons of support, so I was pleased that I had not gone with the other UK person and signed up instead with her. I believe that things are always put in front of you in such a way that you pay attention if it is the right thing for you. After all the synchronicity I knew this was the way forward, but it did not end there.

The very same day I was chatting to someone in my local park where I was walking my dogs when another lady came over to join in the conversation. She said it was the same product that she was to travel 30 mins to collect from someone that she had seen advertising it. She said now that I was a distributor, she could buy from me. I put a note on Facebook and was very surprised to find my sister in Jersey was using it. I knew that this was not only the right product for my skin, but also a way for me to make that additional stream of income. Synchronicity is all around us if we are only aware as to what we are being shown. Interesting to know that in the end I decided it was not in my nature to sell extra products at that time, so I decided just to buy the products for me instead. I did know though that something was going to be put into my life in the future. I never doubted that.

My job during the day was with an energy company helping vulnerable customers. One of the things we gave away was called The Warm Home discount. After we assessed people for this money, we read a legal script out to them which says they must still be on supply with us to receive the payment. As it was the start of a new year, I was given the new scripting to use. When I read it to a customer for the first time, I saw a £ sign behind the printed words which had been laminated. I thought this was great as every day I read out the scripting about thirty times, so each time I was able to envisage money coming to me as well as to the customers. This was given to me a month before the other things above happened. It was a good way of reinforcing my thoughts. The interesting thing was, after checking my team members laminates, mine was the only one with the £ sign. How good was that!

Another synchronistic thing happened. I had a blog and I was updating it but wishing I had someone to tell me if I should change the way I was working it. The same day I looked on Facebook at a page I am a member of and guess what? A Blogging expert was offering free tuition for an hour on how to blog! I loved chatting with her and learned so much from our conversation. One of these was that my blogs did not need to be so detailed as long as they were interesting!

On the same page there was a life coach who had been given homework by her coach to chat to 100 people for an hour each. I thought it would be interesting to sign up for this and came away with so much information to help me both personally and in my business. Talk about being in the right place at the right time.

Many people don't like Facebook. In these days of getting information instantly it is up with the internet and my kindle and I have had loads of synchronicity through using it.

One day I had ordered a book on Kindle that was written by someone I am a friend of on Facebook. He was someone introduced to
me by the Skellee author AnneMarie Callan. I happened to look on
his page where he was talking about it coming out on paper for-
mat soon too. I mentioned that Amazon advised me it would be
delivered to my Kindle 4 days later. It was already available in the
Amazon.com so the UK was a little later. Within 5 minutes I had a
Facebook message from the author with an almost final PDF copy
of his book so that I could read it then rather than having to wait.
How great was that? This wonderful man is called Dr Mani and he
is a children's Heart Surgeon in India. He writes books so that he
can raise funds to operate for free on the children. If you want to
help him, you can find him at https://www.drmani.com

I must admit that getting things instantly can be a curse also in
today's times. Many people have lost the art of patience and get
upset if they must wait for anything. This can be queues in the
supermarket or can be the cause of road rage whilst driving. I had
a student who advised me he did a lot of driving for his work and
was prone to road rage. After his level Two reiki workshop I set
him some homework to reduce this. I suggested giving himself
reiki before setting off on his journey and if he felt the annoyance
building up to concentrate on energy working through him to
calm him down. When I saw him four weeks later the road rage
had decreased by 70%. He was working on the remaining 30%.
How I love reiki. It can be used in so many situations.

I love when synchronicity affects my friends too. I had a friend
staying with me for a week and we were visiting places that she
wanted to see as well as visiting events at the Edinburgh Festi-
val. I left my friend talking to one of the guides at one destination. When I returned, she advised she had spoken to the guide

about craft work she did. The guide said his wife did the same, so she showed him some photographs of her work. He thought they were brilliant and when she asked if she could copy some things to replicate, he suggested to her to make them for this historical site. Even more synchronicity, as earlier that day she had been saying that rather than taking a lot of time to do projects for individuals, she wanted to do work that she could replicate! She was also one of my students and trained in reiki. I think it was a very quick response to advising her that same morning to put her thoughts out there.

My award-winning Wedding planner friend had some more synchronicity happen to her. As her business had taken off so quickly and she has people from all over the world asking her to help plan their special day, she said her aim was to have her own venue. I said to put it out there and it would happen. Not four weeks later a stranger called her. He said he was a farmer and had a couple of barns that were not used. Having been to a couple of weddings recently he knew barns were popular venues. My friend arranged a visit, but they did not gel with her. The farmer then said he had a farm also for sale. He took her to visit it and she fell in love with it. The interesting thing is everything was going well when suddenly road blocks were put in the way from a few directions. She pulled out of this and immediately was contacted by someone else with a better suggestion. I think she is now in so much demand by other venues that she may not have the time to even search for her venue. She is happy though and that is all that matters.

It really is amazing how much what we put out there comes back to us. A friend of mine wanted to relocate to Scotland but secretly really wanted a job to be in Edinburgh. She had no sooner put it out there when she was granted an interview from an agency to work in Edinburgh. She knew that she was having problems getting a property to rent because of having a dog. In her dreams she wanted to live by the sea but was resigned to living wherever she could take her dog. She saw that we have a lot of the sea around us and put it out there to get a place to rent along the sea front if possible. She got her flat with a lovely landlord who told her to make the flat into a long-term home for them both. All she needs do now is open her back door and walk to the beach. She can also look out her kitchen window and see the beach. She couldn't have got any closer to the beach.

One of the job interviews that she really felt most comfortable in had large white feathers as wings in an open fireplace. She had messed up the timing and almost missed the interview, so we had a chat while she got ready as the person interviewing decided to wait on her. I sent reiki for her and told her to take a taxi to the interview to give her some time to calm down. As the interview was two days before the date she had pencilled in, she was worried she had not studied enough for the job. She was amazed to find that during the conversation with the taxi driver he was giving her some of the answers. In the end she got the job! She said that as soon as she saw the feathers a good feeling had come over her. She could also feel the reiki energy that I was sending to her working.

White feathers are often seen as a message from the Angels for people. The other interesting point is we were in a Buddhist Monastery garden when she received the call to say she had the job. We had gone there and were sitting by the water which has a lovely stream which then forks into two. We had been talking about which direction her life was taking. If you ever get the chance to visit somewhere like that, it is so peaceful and relaxing. I have also trained this friend to reiki level two as well. Can you see a trend here?

MY SUPER SEVEN CRYSTALS

I love dragons. I love reading stories about them including crystal dragons. One day I saw on Facebook that a friend who imports crystals, including dragons, was showing a photo of one. She said to check her website for more so, of course, I had to peek. Now the interesting thing is just the day before, I was holding a Super Seven attunement crystal, and it came into my head to see if there was any jewellery made with the stone. Guess what I found when I went on her website? Not one, but two fantastic pieces of Super Seven jewellery. There was a pendant plus a bracelet. Even at half price, they were more than I could afford. I then checked a few other sites and found smaller, cheaper ones were available. On asking why hers were more expensive, the word given was quality. I hummed and hawed, not being able to decide which one to go for. She then told me I could pay it up. The interesting thing was a few months before I had been burgled. All my special pieces of jewellery were stolen, and I had made a promise to myself that I would never have anything expensive again. She told me to stop thinking that way. Well, I then decided to take both! I knew I was getting a bonus in a few days so would then be able to pay half and agreed over the next two months to clear it in full. I was then thinking, if she could just knock another £50 off, I would feel more comfortable with the price. Unbelievably she then said, "Because it's you, I'm going to deduct £50!" I was once again blow away with how the Universe works, but that was not the end of it.

When I came off chatting with her there was an email to say someone had paid for a reiki workshop that I had not been expecting. This enabled me to send her a payment immediately. A few days later when I received my bonus, I could not understand why it was higher than I was expecting. I then realised that a pay increase had been backdated a few months. Guess what I was able to do? I paid it off in full, less than a week after I had decided to buy. It meant that a few days later I received both pieces of jewellery which I love. I can see why I could not decide. An interesting thing happened when I opened the parcel. I decided, as with all new crystals, that I would cleanse them with reiki. I took the pendant out of the bag it was in and felt this coolness go all the way up my back, killing the pain I was in. The Universe certainly decided I needed it sooner rather than later, don't you think?

Another lovely piece of dragon synchronicity came my way when I went to a Networking meetup with a group of therapists. I was telling them that I had just received delivery of a large dragon made of clay. It was much smaller than the one I had wanted, which had sold out, but I instantly fell in love with it. We were talking about me wanting to write a book and one lady told us she had been on an Amazon Workday to learn all about writing. She had lots to inform us about. She then said to me at the end of the discussion, "I'm a dragon too". I looked at her, confused. She then told me she was born in the year of the dragon. It did not end there as I met her again a couple of years later at a meetup group and she offered to give me feedback on my book!

DOGS AND REIKI

The interesting thing with my dogs, who are now both attuned to reiki, is I now allow them to stay during my workshops. There have been a couple of times when people said their breathing has changed while I have been doing a meditation. True enough I have recorded it and when I tell people to take deep slow breaths, I can see both the dogs doing it too. I now call them my reiki dogs. Willow got her wish and has become a therapy dog as both allow students to give them one to one and distance reiki. Especially for distance reiki, it's good for the students to see when the dogs decide it's over, as they often feel the energy stop at that same time.

More recently my daughter asked me to attune her very nervous collie cross. He is the most lovable, cuddly dog but was very reactive. Sometimes he would even react to statues in the street. He had become worse since his companion had passed away due to tetanus. As he came to spend a day with me, I attuned him. It was a beautiful experience as he sat in front of me with his head bowed and allowed me to lift his paw when required. She then advised me that the first two days he was worse and then he calmed and stopped barking at things he usually got upset at. Success! I have now been asked to attune a friend's dog, so I will see how that goes. I'm sure that dogs as well as people can have a little healing crisis after being attuned to reiki. Often students love to go home after a course and give their animals reiki. Most will accept it but not all. Don't be disheartened- remember Misty who chose when she was ready.

One important thing about reiki, you can be standing next to someone and find the energy switching on. It usually means the person beside you needs to be balanced in some way. Never do what someone did to me years ago. I was at a mother and toddlers' group, with my childminded children, after my marriage had broken up, and a lady came up to me. She put her hands on my shoulders and said, "You need this". I had no idea what she was doing, and it freaked me out. Yes, reiki is always with you, but please ask permission before you give it to another person. There are a couple of instances when you can give reiki without permission. This can be if someone is in a coma or near to death. Reiki will only be accepted by the person if their Higher Self accepts it too. You can also send it over distance to situations such as war zones. Of course, in that circumstance, permission is not required either. Animals also have a higher self and you will be shown quickly if they wish to receive distance reiki or not.

GRATITUDE

One of the things I have learned over the years is to be grateful for what is in my life. I make it my goal to think of three things I am grateful for every night before bed. It can help to write these down. That way, if you are having an off day, it can help you remember all the good things in the preceding days. Even if something feels off and not right for you at a point, you will often find on looking back that it needed to happen for you to get to where you are now. In fact, one morning I woke up and these words came into my head which I will share with you now. Just to let you know, I have never written a poem, so no laughs please.

The Gratitude Poem
I looked out of the window. The sun was shining bright.
The clouds were still in the sky, but everything was alright.
The weather can be fickle but, in our hearts, it's true,
we do not need the weather to stop us feeling blue.

Our feelings come from us inside.
It's up to us you see, to make sure that every day we get the time for you and me.
There are things all around us that open our hearts with love, like trees and plants and butterflies and not forgetting what comes from above.

These are things that bring peace to our lives in these days of war and strife.
There are also many other things to make us grateful for our life. When you wake up in the morning, where are you in your mind?
It's up to you to choose this best and it starts with being kind.

Being kind to others lifts both them and you.

It's a gift we can give for free, that benefits us all, that's true. Paying it Forward can help in this way and it's very easy to do.
Just use your eyes and your ears each day and see where your help is needed.
It then comes back full circle to you when you find that you have succeeded.

Filling your heart with Love and Gratitude is surely the way to go to help you start your day off right and really get in the flow.
Your mind can really work wonders, in setting you up for the day, so use it now to expand your life as you continue along the way.

This is a great way to start your day. Irrespective of who you meet, always remember, you have a choice how you communicate back. Learn to be grateful for what surrounds you. It may be a roof over your head, food on the table, flowers in the garden and family too. If you think about it, you will find lots of things you too can celebrate in your life.

PAYING IT FORWARD

Many years ago, I was introduced to Paying it Forward. This was started from a book by Catherine Ryan Hyde. You should check it out. The rules of PIF are just to help someone in any way without expecting anything in return. It reminded me of The Free Economy. It could be that you get a work colleague a cup of coffee he was not expecting or helping someone at the checkout who perhaps did not have enough money. I remember reading that someone at a fast food drive through said she would pay for the person next in lines food. This filtered through the line and was repeated many times.

In Edinburgh we have a great café that opened called Social Bite. They asked people who were buying coffee or food to leave money to pay for something to allow homeless people to eat or drink also. I agree that today we should have no homeless but at least it was a start. People signed up in their droves and made it so successful that they have expanded to other Scottish cities. They are now on target from massive fundraising to get people permanently off the streets. In 2018 they opened the Social Bite Village, which is a collection of tiny homes for the homeless to live. A lot of synchronicity happened during this time and Social Bite started employing homeless people off the streets to work with them. Well done to them and all the people that slept outside in Edinburgh's Princes Street Gardens on the coldest night of 2017 to raise thousands of pounds. The next year they arranged to have a sleep out being held in a few different cities in Scotland all on the same night. This meant they would have celebrities getting on a plane to travel from one location to the next to entertain

Joy Fraser

those sleeping outside.

EAMONN'S FUNDRAISING

In 2014 my grandson Eamonn decided to do a fun thing. It was called Eamonn's Trading Project. It came about as on the last day of term the teacher had been telling the class about Kyle Mac-Donald who traded up from a red paperclip to a house. On the first day back to school guess what Eamonn found? That's right – a red paperclip. He went home and told his dad the story of Kyle, and Eamonn decided to try this out too. His father set him up with a Facebook page to advertise it.

On the second day he visited me and decided he would do it for charity. He ended up with a prize worth a few hundred pounds, but he was not content with that. He decided to run a fun day at his local centre. He went around many shops and got them to give raffle prizes. He then had face painters, magicians, nail technicians, the local fire brigade and lots of stalls with people selling things. He made a lot of money from all his fundraising. The charity to receive this was his local food bank. Eamonn said it was his way of paying back as they had helped his family in the past. When he started on his fundraiser journey, he was only ten years old. He became a local celebrity and was in the newspapers and radio stations.

After seeing what Social Bite was doing three years later, Eamonn decided to raise funds for hats and gloves for the homeless. He had been in town during the summer and gave a homeless person some of his lunch. He thought about what they would do during the coldness of winter and was very concerned about this. I set up a funding page for him as now he was thirteen years of age. I seemed to have trouble getting people to donate, possibly because Social Bite was advertising a lot and many people were donating to that. I then listened to a radio station that was interviewing a couple of people I know so emailed the presenter. She aired on Tuesdays when I was at work, so I usually played catch up online and listened to her later in the week.

This week I had stopped two dogs fighting and my back went so I was unable to work. She messaged me on my first day sick and then asked me to go on the show by calling in and speaking about the fundraiser. As I knew I would be still off the next day I said that I would love to do this. See synchronicity really does work in mysterious ways. In the end we managed to buy eighty sets of gloves and hats and gave these to a charity who went out on the streets to feed and give shelter to the homeless.

I always remember when Eamonn was about three years old and he saw something on television about collecting toys for children and to box them up and send to their destination. Unknown to his Mum he went upstairs and collected handfuls of toys and brought them downstairs. He then asked his mum for a box. He really does have a heart of gold.

TRAINING CHILDREN

Two of the greatest experiences I ever had were training my grandchildren in reiki. All through Eamonn's life he kept asking me to train him in reiki. Up to a point he thought that he would be able to go into the school playground and say "Kapow!" Although reiki is great to play around with, I do draw the line at that. I had advised him that when mum said it was the correct time, I would be honoured to train him. When he eventually said the reason he wanted to learn was to help my daughter when she was in pain, we both knew he was ready to learn reiki. Even better we agreed to train my granddaughter too. She loves to listen to meditation, and I was sure she was in the right frame of mind even though she is younger than her brother.

Before this I had never thought of training any children, so I spoke to two teachers I knew online. One told me that she had trained children who had ADHD, Autism, Separation Anxiety after parents split up or had even died. She told me how much it had helped the children. I remember one story she told me. A boy was in the car with his parents and his CD started jumping and not playing correctly. Usually, his parents advised, he would freak out and get very angry. This time he told them the CD needed reiki and applied it with his hands. He then sat back, relaxed, as it continued to play without any problems. His parents were astounded at the changes in him. I decided to plan out a day to train both my Grandchildren. I also added in a friend's fourteen-year-old who was unhappy with all the bullying she was getting at school.

After the children's' workshop my grandchildren went outdoor camping. My granddaughter, who was eight at the time, couldn't wait to see me when they came back. She excitedly told me that when she felt angry, she went and sat on a rock and gave herself reiki. She also told me if she was upset in the bedroom she sat and gave herself reiki till she felt better. This was such a breakthrough for her. My friend's daughter did not even realise that she went back to school after Summer with her head held up high. She has changed so much since that day.

A couple of years later there was the possibility of my daughter going into hospital further away. The children were concerned that they would not be able to visit her as often, so I decided to train them to level two. Mum says it has made such a difference to them both. Then I asked my granddaughter Chloe if she would like to paint a fence for me. Of course, I was going to give her money for doing it. She advised me she would do it for a hug. I think a hug for a good few hours work is a great deal for me, but she got a nice surprise too. Chloe is also my first person to assess any children's meditations I record. Both her and Eamonn heard the first one and told me to sell it! This was my next learning curve. I have since made a few which you will be able to find a couple of them on my YouTube page and shortly they will be on sale from my website. I am looking forward to making personal meditation videos and children's story videos. The children's ones have passed the grandchildren test!

Another piece of synchronicity happened when my daughter was in two hospitals. In one of them she had a book by her bed. A nurse saw it and said she knew someone who was friends with the author. My daughter said," So does my mum". They worked out they were both talking about the same person, me. I had trained the nurse in reiki. In another hospital I was visiting her and another of my students came in and realised she was my daughter. I think she got well looked after. After that I said my plan was to train someone in each hospital she may have to go to!

IF YOU WANT TO LEARN REIKI

At this time reiki is not regulated but that is in the process of being addressed. If you are looking to be trained in reiki, start as you mean to go on and research who you wish to be trained by. I would usually suggest going and chatting to or having a therapy session with the teacher to see if he/she feels right for you. Although reiki is spiritual it is not religious and is open to everyone. After the attunement the student has access to an unlimited supply of Life force energy. It is with you for life. I remember a student who had trained many years ago and never used reiki on herself. She had an accident on holiday and wondered if it would help. To her surprise, the reiki started flowing.

When thinking of choosing a teacher you need to know what you want from him/her. Ask yourself these questions: -

- What do I want from Reiki?
- Do I want the facility of on-going support?
- What is the cost?
- What is included i.e.: Manuals, certificates, handouts, refreshments
- What are the maximum sizes for a class?
- Is training on a One to One basis available and at what cost?
- Is the location suitable?
- Check the Master / Teacher certificates and that the person is insured.

Don't be afraid to request contact details of a couple of people that have trained with the teacher. See if there are any testimonials on the teacher's website.

Reiki is the best thing I ever did for myself. If I had known the blessings and synchronicities it would bring into my life, I would have learned years ago.

This book started off all about synchronicity and reiki, but on looking back it shows synchronicity is now in so many parts of my life. Sometimes it surprises me how often it occurs in my life. Reiki opens your intuition and makes you so much more aware of things and open to changes in your life, so I just accept wherever life takes me.

Even part of the writing of this book was down to Synchronicity. I had bought a programme to allow me to convert my word document into a Kindle book. I knew that I would not be using it immediately as I did not have the time. Instead I decided to use it n month later when I had a week's holiday from work. Now I don't know if you are aware that Scotland had not been having much sunshine during our last few Summers. Well this year we have had glorious sunshine every day for weeks. I knew I had to make the most of the sun, so was out visiting attractions every day of my holidays, instead of using the programme I had purchased. My next Holiday was two months away, so I thought it would just have to wait. I did not have to wait that long though as my back went and I was signed off sick. At this point my friend said she thought this was the Universe telling me to sit down and get on with writing my book! So, of course, I did. I then decided to leave work earlier than I had anticipated so now have time at my disposal to do more writing as well!

As I have walked my journey with reiki, I have been learning all the way through it. I now know that not only people but also animals, children, plants and so much more can all be helped by reiki. You can send it to situations, into the past and future but most of all you also learn to live in the now. The best present you can give yourself is to enjoy where you are at now. Don't keep looking back to the past and don't keep wishing for the future. Use the present to make changes for the future of course but enjoy whatever you choose to do.

I hope you have enjoyed my little story of reiki and synchronicities. I started out saying I wanted to call this the never-ending story. It truly is, as synchronicity will flow through us until we die. I have had hundreds of events that I always meant to write down and have forgotten, probably because I now accept them just as part of my life. You may be thinking those in your life are just coincidences. All I say, is be open to being aware when these things happen and see if they are synchronistic instead. Thank you for listening to my muses. I hope I have encouraged some of you to investigate learning reiki or even going for a therapy session. You will not look back once you let reiki into your life.

NAMASTE

I wish to thank all my friends and relatives who have allowed me to write about them. A special thanks go to Lorraine Fiander for sending me the Celestine prophecy and keeping me on track. Thanks also to Beata Dziamecka for my lovely cover photo that was taken at Silverknowes Beach, Edinburgh.

Printed in Great Britain
by Amazon

61176658R00064